ULYSSES

The Mechanics of Meaning

ULYSSES

The Mechanics of Meaning

DAVID HAYMAN

A new edition, revised and expanded

The University of Wisconsin Press

Published 1982

The University of Wisconsin Press
114 North Murray Street
Madison, Wisconsin 53715

The University of Wisconsin Press, Ltd.
1 Gower Street
London WC1E 6HA, England

The first edition of *"ULYSSES": The Mechanics of Meaning*
was published by Prentice-Hall, Inc., in 1970.

Printed in the United States of America

For LC CIP information see the colophon

ISBN 0-299-09020-5 cloth; 0-299-09024-8 paper

Acknowledgment is made to the following publishers for permission to reprint excerpts in this book: From *Finnegans Wake* by James Joyce. Copyright 1939 by James Joyce, renewed 1967 by George Joyce and Lucia Joyce. Reprinted by permission of The Viking Press, Inc. From *A Portrait of the Artist as a Young Man* by James Joyce. Copyright 1916 by B. W. Huebsch, Inc., renewed 1944 by Nora Joyce. Copyright 1964 by the Estate of James Joyce. All rights reserved. Reprinted by permission of The Viking Press, Inc. From *Ulysses* by James Joyce. Copyright 1914, 1918 by Margaret Caroline Anderson and renewed 1942, 1946 by Nora Joseph Joyce. Reprinted by permission of Random House, Inc. The Joyce schema and pages 37 and 86 from Notebook VI.B.10 are reprinted by permission of the Society of Authors on behalf of the Trustees of the Estate of James Joyce.

. . . his usylessly unreadable Blue Book of Eccles, *édition de ténèbres,* (even yet sighs the Most Different, Dr. Poindejenk, authorised bowdler and censor, it can't be repeated!) . . .

Finnegans Wake

Contents

Preface

The present edition of *"Ulysses": The Mechanics of Meaning* has been thoroughly revised for both style and the correction of minor errors. I am grateful to the critics of the first edition for pointing the latter out to me. Though there are no major alterations to the text proper, I have added in appendix, as an aid for the beginning reader, a concise guide to the action of each chapter, of *Ulysses*. To complete the critical picture, I have also appended some revisions and extensions of positions elaborated in the text, fruits of ten years of further work on *Ulysses*. I should like to thank Julián Ríos, Bernard Benstock, Hugh Kenner, and my wife, Loni, for help and encouragement.

1981

Preface
to the 1970 Edition

A glance at the imposing Joyce bibliography, the acres of words, the conflicting critical positions and varied approaches, the secondary sources and documents, especially such monuments as Richard Ellmann's 800-page biography and the three volumes of letters, will convince anyone that little can be said in a hundred pages about James Joyce's *Ulysses*. But then perhaps we have surrounded the monster with a wall that can still be breached by a modest volume designed to serve the general reader as a descriptive introduction.

There is no room in a book of this sort for a review of critical positions or a rehash of long established "facts" or a careful summary of the action. Instead, I would refer interested readers to some of the books listed in my bibliography. Neither is there room for a full consideration of the relationship of Ireland and Joyce's life to his work or of the function of his theories. The latter have, in my opinion, been taken too seriously by those who would make youthful pronouncements into manifestos and too lightly by those who would have the works spring into being without intellectual bases or literary forebears. For my own part I assume that Joyce's works grow naturally out of literary traditions fostered by the European nineteenth century.

Aiming at the presentation of an integral sense of the novel with an assessment of Joyce's accomplishment and the role of *Ulysses* in his work and in our century, I have deliberately stressed form as it relates to content. It is my conviction that Joyce's contribution is twofold: he has created (1) a most lifelike situation in (2) a most delightful manner. At the risk of seeming mechanical and even pedestrian I have chosen to consider in turn *Ulysses'* action, characters, and setting, the thematic uses of analogy, and the application of paradox, and then the techniques, the structure, and the styles as functional aspects of the book's meaning. Along the way I have stressed certain themes and motifs and attempted to show how through them the book develops the situations of its chief personae. I believe that this approach will suggest the sort of questions one can ask of *Ulysses* and the sort of answers one may expect to get.

I have placed in appendix a copy of the much-reproduced schema for *Ulysses,* a suggestive document which can be used as a partial index to the author's sense of the book but not as a definitive key to its many aspects. Following tradition, I have used Joyce's homeric chapter headings, assuming the presence of analogies discussed in my chapter IV. I have also assumed that the reader will be familiar with both *The Odyssey* and *A Portrait of the Artist as a Young Man.*

ULYSSES

The Mechanics of Meaning

I

Backgrounds

Historical Contexts

James Joyce called *Finnegans Wake* the book of "Doublends Jined." *Ulysses* is the book of Dublin. Dublin is conceived to be an anagram for Ireland, and Ireland to be an aspect of universal history, every detail of which is important (but also impotent) in the general scheme of the universe created by a God who may have been very much like "Jeems Joker" himself. But appearances to the contrary, neither Dublin nor Ireland is a figment of the Joycean imagination.

The Ireland that Leopold Bloom feels is important because he wishes to belong to it and that Stephen Dedalus values because it belongs to him was not always the cultural backwater depicted by Joyce in *Ulysses,* a country praising its own past, a land whose best and most valuable export is "wild geese" and artists, who fight, each in his way, on foreign soil. Its history goes back into the night of prehistory whence successive waves of invaders came, conquered, settled, and left their marks even before the Romans invaded and reinvaded Britain. Irish recorded history is as turbulent as the shadowy past of Parthalons, Firbolgs, the fabulous Tuatha Dedanaan, and the sons of Milesius or the Milesians of whom Joyce's citizen-Cyclops is so proud and whose tales were being rewritten and romanticized by significant as well as "paltryattic" writers during Joyce's youth. The annals Joyce used so extensively in *Finnegans Wake* tell of quarrelsome men, tribal wars, meaningless victories and defeats, invasions, natural disasters, or, as Ste-

3

phen sees it reflected in the play of small boys at Deasy's school, self-perpetuating carnage:

> Again: a goal. I am among them, among their battling bodies in a medley, the joust of life . . . Jousts. Time shocked rebounds, shock by shock. Jousts, slush and uproar of battles, the frozen deathspew of the slain, a shout of spear spikes baited with men's bloodied guts. (32)[1]

Also buried in prehistory are the Celtic bards and priests or Olavs of the Druids, children of a highly articulate people which built few permanent monuments but created tales and spells that survived the first historical conquest, Saint Patrick's fifth century spiritual victory in the name of Jesus Christ when, as Joyce comically puts it in *Finnegans Wake:*

> . . . he converted it's nataves . . . through the medium of znigznaks with sotiric zeal, to put off the barcelonas . . . and kiss on their bottes (Master!) as often as they came within bloodshot of that other familiar temple . . .[2]

During the early middle ages Irish monks founded monastic communities amidst warring Irish tribes, or went out as missionaries into a turbulent and barbaric Europe to establish islands of culture. This period, perhaps the greatest of Irish history, was punctuated by the Viking forays of the ninth century, but, turning gradually from piracy to trade, the alien Galls built the first permanent cities on the seacoast, towns like Dublin, Galway, Waterford, Wexford, and Cork. A new era came when a handful of Norman knights led by Richard de Clare were invited to settle a quarrel between two Irish chieftains caused by what Mr. Deasy calls "a woman no better than she should be." The Normans settled Ireland in the name of Henry II, carving up the available land, becoming more Irish than English, leaving behind names like Fitzgerald and Joyce (Josse). Thanks to a papal bull, the *"Bos Bovum"* of which so much bitter fun is made in *Ulysses'* "Oxen of the Sun," Ireland was nominally under the English crown, but the invasions and repressions ordered by Elizabeth I, Cromwell, and William of Orange were required to remind the restless natives of this fact.

Partly as a result of the repressions, Catholicism, which was virtually eliminated in England, continued to flourish, though with-

out official recognition, in an Ireland ruled by members of a Protestant establishment which was strongest in the "Orange" north.
Politically, the Catholic majority was disenfrachised until the middle of the nineteenth century, but in the eighteenth century it
joined in an uneasy alliance with the Protestants and contributed
to the abortive revolution of 1798 which ended the Irish Parliament and brought about the Act of Union with England. After further agitation came the enfranchisement of the Catholics (1829), a
real victory for an alleged relative of Joyce's father, Daniel O'Con-
nell.[3] A repressed and depressed Ireland with a growing population but no industry, no trade, no self-government, suffered its
greatest catastrophe in 1847, when the potato blight brought star-
vation and emigration, halving the mid-century population and
turning the emerald island into a Celtic Zion. The famine, a result
of years of deprivation and English mismanagement, led to increased unrest, violence, and repression.

Thirty years later, during Gladstone's government, Ireland began to move toward the peaceful attainment of Home Rule. The
great leader was an Irish Protestant, Charles Stewart Parnell, who
managed to unite the Irish members of the London Parliament as
an obstructive body capable of exacting compromises from the ruling party. Irish stubbornness under his brilliant leadership became
a powerful weapon. Meanwhile, the Land League, founded by
Parnell and Michael Davitt (1879), agitated for land reform, using
boycotts and occasionally violence, and supported by secret orga-
nizations like the Fenians, White Boys, Molly Maguires, and Rib-
bonmen. Since, for the English, the obstructive Parnell and this
violence were one, it is no wonder that the "inevitable betrayer"
appeared to produce forged letters linking Parnell to the political
assassinations committed by a group called the Invincibles. Parnell
was tried and acquitted, but another betrayer appeared, Captain
O'Shea, a Parnell aide and the husband of his long-time mistress.
Named in O'Shea's divorce suit, Parnell was deposed as a leader
and denounced by the Catholic church. Having suffered at the
hands of his former friends and lost the support of the Irish people,
he died brokenhearted in a divided country. It was this development (which darkens Stephen Dedalus' first Christmas dinner in *A
Portrait of the Artist as a Young Man*) that effectively squelched Home
Rule, giving rise to further Fenian agitation, the Irish Language

revival, the literary renaissance, and the Sinn Fein movement, all of which contributed to the revolution and the "troubles" and led eventually to the establishment of the Irish Free State.

Such are the bare bones of the Irish "nightmare" of history from which the depressed and depleted Stephen of *Ulysses* is "trying to awake." These are the tensions which shaped the Ireland into which Joyce was "lugged," "squealing into life," on February 2, 1882, so that he could grow up the most extraordinary product of the Irish *fin de siècle*. Though it would not do to exaggerate the importance of history in the life of a man who had more in common with the "Irish saints and sages" than with the wild Irish, Joyce too was torn and shaped by conflicting forces: by antagonisms between an international church and a passionate secular nationalism; between an unstable but vital home environment and a stable theological system; between the repressive demands of a culture at once ailing and aspiring and a growing sense of his own worth accompanied by a need to express himself freely; between his strong, pious, long-suffering mother and his wonderfully gifted but profligate father, a man who accumulated debts and children while leading the life of a Dublin character and who always traveled in reasonably good company.

Along with a fine tenor voice, a mimic's ear, and a love of language that are characteristically Irish, Joyce seems to have inherited from his father, a truly fine sense of the word. From his mother he derived a respect for the church and things of the spirit. A shy, proud boy, with quick wit but poor sight, he preferred words to actions and written to oral presentation. He quickly found pleasure in books which led him out of Ireland even before he left the Irish church. Joyce's childhood was marred by the steady decline of his father's fortunes which was manifested in a seemingly endless series of quick moves into increasingly depressing homes. Still, apart from a short period spent with the plebeian Christian Brothers, whom Stephen Dedalus so despised,[4] his training was entirely in the hands of the proud and sophisticated Jesuits, who instilled in him a love of ritual and an astonishing mental discipline.[5] His engagement with the church, which doubtless helped him in his pride to support disappointments elsewhere, was so strong that severance left permanent marks. Inevitably, in his books the church is one of a trinity of insidious enemies and obsessive themes: church, home, country. No wonder Joyce makes the prime motive of Stephen's gloom in *Ulysses* his failure to "kneel down and pray" for his dying mother (an event that has only symbolic significance in terms of his biography).

By the time Joyce graduated from Belvedere College and entered University College, literature had begun to serve as a substitute for a priestly vocation. When he graduated from University College in 1902, Ireland and the Irish literary set were already too small for him. He had read widely in continental literature and may even have begun to cultivate the protective mask described in *A Portrait of the Artist as a Young Man* and *Ulysses*. His first major publication, a critical article, "Ibsen's New Drama" (on *When We Dead Awaken*), published in the prestigious *Fortnightly Review* in 1900 while he was still an undergraduate, had established him among his classmates as something of a phenomenon. Drawing heavily on Aquinas, Aristotle, Shelley, Flaubert, and Pater, he had begun to formulate an esthetic that spoke for a discipline in his art equivalent to that of the monk in his belief and helped shape his early work, pointing him toward the later experiments. The actual composition of that esthetic (reproduced in large measure in *Stephen Hero* and somewhat altered for *A Portrait of the Artist as a Young Man*)[6] took place mainly in Paris where he went ostensibly to study medicine. After a short hungry stay during which he read Ben Jonson and Aristotle and picked up current fads, he was called back to Dublin, in April 1903, to his mother's deathbed. (She died of cancer in August, almost ten months before the day of *Ulysses*.) Still hungry, Joyce remained in Dublin to witness her decline, writing, teaching, carousing with his friends, quarreling with his father, and courting Nora Barnacle, the semiliterate provincial who later became his wife. Always a date-fetishist (his books characteristically appeared on his birthday, February the second), he memorialized the day of his first date with Nora, June 16, 1904, as the day of *Ulysses*. It was during this transitional period that, casting about like Stephen for means of support, Joyce took singing lessons and even performed in several concerts, failing to win the gold medal at the Irish Festival of Music or Feis Ceoil only because he could not sight read. Finally, in October, after a short wild stay in the Martello tower with Oliver St. John Gogarty, Joyce ran off with Nora to Zurich and settled with her in Trieste. He had promised his friends to produce a novel in fifteen years, one which would surely not make him popular in Dublin.[7] Though he returned for two brief turbulent visits (1909, 1912), Joyce was effectively in permanent, self-imposed exile.

Before leaving Ireland the second time, Joyce had published, under the pseudonym Stephen Daedalus, the first three of his laconic but biting stories for *Dubliners*. He had also composed poems for his first book, *Chamber Music*, fluty love songs in the Elizabethan manner inspired partly by Ben Jonson but probably also by the French *décadent* poet Paul Verlaine. Both songs and tales jibed with the tastes of the Dublin literati though neither suggested the direction his later work would take. More important was the biographical essay, "A Portrait of the Artist," written early in 1904 and refused for publication by the editor of *Dana*, John Eglinton, who was unwilling to print anything he could not understand. The refusal was fortunate, for Joyce turned then to the second and immensely more elaborate version which he continued to work on during the first two years of his European exile. *Stephen Hero,* as this work in progress was ironically entitled, was a detailed and largely factual account of Joyce's own development. Its protagonist was given the name of the "fabulous artificer" Daedalus, who built the labyrinth for King Minos of Crete and later escaped the island on wings of wax and feathers. Stephen is predestined by his nature to become such a figure, the elaborator of great and original literary work, but at this point he is more like Icarus, a clumsy but gifted fledgling, too eager to try his wings.

In 1904, when he left Ireland, where he had suffered poverty and ego damage but failed to make much of a mark, Joyce was already on his way as a writer. Nevertheless, it was his faith in himself that sustained him during the early years of his exile in Trieste where he eventually summoned three members of his family (his brother Stanislaus and two of his sisters). There, while teaching English at the Berlitz school or giving private lessons, he published *Chamber Music* with help from Arthur Symons, finished *Dubliners* (in 1907), and fought the publishers and printers, who persisted in finding objectionable material in the stories, which were finally published in 1914 after many alarms and skirmishes. In 1907, after abandoning *Stephen Hero*, Joyce began rewriting his youth as *A Portrait of the Artist as a Young Man*, a highly stylized, internally focussed, and richly symbolic *Bildungsroman*. For all of this activity and despite his frustrations and straitened means, these were tranquil years given over to hard and fruitful work and to the raising of two children, Georgio and Lucia.

In the crucial year 1906, during a brief unhappy interlude as a bank clerk in Rome, which he hated as much as he seems to have loved Trieste, Joyce had an idea. He would write a story for *Dubliners* about a traveling man named Hunter, a Dublin Jew whose wife was said to be unfaithful.[8] Had it been written then, "Ulysses" would have been a slight and probably satirical outsider's view of the "seventh city of Christendom," certainly not an experimental earth shaker. Still, *Ulysses* can be thought of as the last and greatest tale in *Dubliners,* the full-scale portrait designed to convey the beauty and squalor of a city to which the writer could not return but which he could never get out of his head.

In 1915, during World War I, Joyce left Austro-Hungarian Trieste for neutral Switzerland. In the course of the previous year and almost simultaneously, he had completed *A Portrait of the Artist as a Young Man,* begun *Ulysses,* and written his play *Exiles.* The latter treats, somewhat in the vein of Ibsen, the return of a writer very much like Joyce to an Ireland that has previously disowned him but now recognizes his success. The play is mainly concerned, however, with the willed but problematical cuckolding of the returned writer, Richard Rowan, by his best friend and admirer, the journalist Robert Hand. Designed to shock a turn-of-the-century audience with its moral and sexual audacities, it is poor theatre, overloaded with symbolic and thematic significance, full of wooden dialogue and lush ambiguities, and peopled by unconvincing characters. But it is as hard to imagine Joyce writing *Ulysses* without first having written this play as it is to think of *Ulysses* as preceding *A Portrait of the Artist as a Young Man.*

Joyce wrote *Ulysses* largely during the war years in Zurich. In this period, and thanks mainly to the good offices of Ezra Pound, he had already begun to make his reputation through the serial publication of *A Portrait of the Artist as a Young Man* in an English magazine, *The Egoist* (formerly *The New Free Woman*), edited by two ladies, one of whom, Miss Harriet Weaver, became his life-long patroness. After the war, he stayed first in Trieste, where he shared cramped quarters with his brother Stanislaus (a former confidant and one of the models for the anti-Stephen figures). Later he moved to Paris, where, thanks again to Pound, he was almost immediately a celebrity. *Ulysses* was completed while the family shifted from room to Paris room between 1920 and 1922. In the meantime, however, it had begun to appear serially, first in the American *Little Review* and then in *The Egoist,* and had attracted enough attention to be banned in America and England. Its thirteenth chapter, "Nausikaa," was apparently simple enough for the censors to understand. For ten years after its first publication under the imprint of Sylvia Beach's Paris bookstore, Shakespeare and Co., *Ulysses,* a *succès de scandale,* was smuggled into the States by thrill-seeking tourists. Paradoxically (or properly), the book with Molly in it had prospered in the hands of emancipated women. As Joyce puts it in *Finnegans Wake,* things haven't been the same since "Biddy Doran," the hen scratching up filth in a kitchen midden, "looked ad literature."[9]

By 1933, when Judge Woolsey wrote his landmark decision lifting the ban,[10] the world was ready to accept his experiments, but Joyce had already put eleven years' work into a new and more outrageous project. His greatest book, the puzzling "Work in Progress" (finally published as *Finnegans Wake*), began to appear in Paris periodicals in 1924. For nearly eighteen years, during which he was repeatedly operated on for the eye ailment glaucoma, Joyce elaborated like a true latter-day Daedalus a book without beginning or end, with endless strands of meaning and limitless associative possibililties, burrowing, it would seem, deep into the texture of his own psyche to uncover a vast area of shared experience based on the universal nature of each individual moment and the risibility of the human tragedy. When he finally published it in February 1939 (on his birthday), the world was too busy with Hitler to notice what had happened to literature or to see itself in Joyce's polished mirror. After a tedious struggle to get his family into Switzerland and away from the war, the writer died in Zurich of the complications following an ulcer operation.

Literary Contexts

Joyce's place was established with the publication of *Ulysses,* but the significance and stature of that book are still being assessed, its sources and influence disputed. Despite the miles and miles of words written about it, it still defies definition, remaining open to each new reader and susceptible to new approaches. We can spot its sources all over the literary map, but it belongs properly to the flaubertian tradition of literary craftsmanship which was created out of what Joyce called the "classical temper." It reflects a marriage of the tendency toward vivid personal expression and the need to universalize and polish that expression, to create autonomous works. Appropriately, the form is totally adequate to the matter, and ordinary life provides a suitable challenge for the artist. However, Joyce goes further than his predecessors in expressing uncompromising honesty and an ironic sensibility, in paying meticulous attention to detail, and in careful management of esthetic distance. (It is incidentally precisely these qualities which have won Joyce enemies among the anti-esthetic camp, the admirers of writers like D. H. Lawrence or Henry Miller.) No one before him had been so frank in his treatment of the mental and the physical man, so serious, so unromantic, and so unlecherous. No one had concerned himself with the unexceptional with quite so much grace, intelligence, and ingenuity. Joyce presents in *Ulysses* a surface that is completely and devastatingly recognizable but which points relentlessly to a deeper sort of recognition, and insists on the universals underlying the objectively presented particulars. Beneath his humor and irony, the trivia of the existences he depicts, and the multiplicity of his effects is an unflagging and undogmatic faith in the human potential and a joy, mixed with equal amounts of sorrow and disgust, in the manifold aspects of our experience. Beyond this is the imaginative vitality of a man in love with words and engaged by the literary traditions with and against which he works.

Of course Joyce saw the turning century, lived through World

War I, and watched distractedly, but with an eye out for raw materials, the liberated twenties which in their turn ushered in inflation, depression, and fascism. But little in his books would suggest that his post-1912 experiences did more than confirm him in his creative direction. In *Finnegans Wake,* in many ways the most personal of his novels, he presents profiles of friends and family, makes reference to the facts of his own later biography, to the literary history of his time, and the current history of Ireland; yet increasingly we sense a detachment from world events and a commitment to the revision of the not-too-distant past. Given the fact that each of his books suggests a different age of man and fresh depths of experience, it is almost as though Joyce had grown old in Dublin, in 1904, the year of his frozen mirror.

If the world was seemingly doing little to effect his shape while he was making literary history, he was never completely isolated from literary events, least of all during his formative years. A product, despite himself, of the Irish nineties, Joyce was marked by the Dublin literary movement which he dismissed as provincial saying in an early essay[11] that George Moore was in a backwater of the realistic movement; spurning Yeats in his Hibernian phase while admiring him as a poet; rejecting the Abbey Theatre as nationalistic; and testing and rejecting the theosophists whom Stephen so cleverly mocks in *Ulysses:* "Through spaces smaller than red globules of man's blood they creepycrawl after Blake's buttocks into eternity of which this vegetable world is but a shadow" (186). For all of this, he was somehow infected by the genuine vigor of a literary atmosphere which was, after all, not wholly provincial. AE (George Russell), like Yeats, popularized an international and archaizing mysticism. Moore and Yeats did help publicize in England and Ireland the works of the French symbolists Joyce at one time admired. Moore was a vociferous exponent of realism and naturalism, a follower of Flaubert as well as Zola. Joyce was proud to come from the land of Swift, Sheridan, Goldsmith, Wilde, Shaw, and Yeats, though he may have been jealously afraid that a Padraic Colum, an Oliver St. John Gogarty, or a J. M. Synge would eclipse him in the eyes of others. In Ireland he deliberately cultivated the pose of the European artist, read the proper periodicals, knew the Russian, Italian, and French novels, read about and in French symbolism, read Dante, Bruno, and D'Annunzio in Italian, learned Dano-Norwegian so that he could read Ibsen in the original, and followed with interest the demise of aestheticism in England. His work reflects all of these tendencies though he wrote entirely out of an Irish awareness, belonged to no movements, steering clear even of Ezra Pound's little band, and, like Flaubert before him, refused to be a *chef d'école*. By the time he began to write, the *fin de siècle* with its wonderful operatic props was something he would react against as did so many of his young contemporaries in France and England; but like Proust, Gide, Claudel, and D. H. Lawrence, he couldn't help reflecting his past any more than he could help rejecting it. We cannot laugh away the earnestness of the young Stephen Dedalus in chapter 5 of *A Portrait of the Artist as a Young Man,* though Joyce makes us smile at the passion with which the neophyte executes a period poem or at the pattern of his emotional crises which reflect on tastes the author has long since rejected (just as Stephen bitterly mocks his own naïve preciosity when he describes his ''epiphanies'' in ''Proteus''). Joyce was untouched however by the earnest Edwardians and the more polished early Georgians. And though he could not ignore the aging giant Henry James, he seems to have preferred to read a florid D'Annunzio even before he left for the continent. By 1915, he was too far advanced in his own relatively well-bred experiments to be touched by the more radical and ephemeral explosions of expressionism, dadaism, or even by the surrealism with which his books have so much in common. For Joyce the psychological experiments of the latter were invalid as art. He was proud that every word of his writing could be justified and doubtless doubly proud of the labyrinthine logic required to achieve such justification.

   Yet, it is no accident that Joyce wrote, in a Zurich full of political, intellectual, and literary tensions which did not directly affect him, a book that was too modern for the twenties. The point is that, while writing increasingly out of himself, he wrote for his contemporaries and reacted as they did to immediate and inescapable pressures. *Ulysses,* a product of his immense detachment from contemporary events, is the inevitable reflection of its times, though fortunately free of the cant that mars products of the programmatic movements. Along with Proust's sprawling *Remembrance of Things Past,* Lawrence's *Sons and Lovers,* Mann's *Magic Mountain,* and Döblin's *Berlin Alexanderplatz,* but more emphatically than any of them, it reflects a digested awareness of intellectual earthquakes and of the coming era of the little man. Though perhaps a trifle too self-consciously, it also reflects an encyclopedic knowledge of the writer's craft and literary conventions. It emerged in 1922 the first completely modern European novel, the most radically experimental, and the most thoroughly conventional: the indigestible but delightful literary banquet that followed the thunderclap that signalled the destruction of an era, preparing us for things to come.

Today, unlike the early readers, we are not likely to be shocked by the obscenity in *Ulysses,* which is after all organic to the work and mild in comparison to the greater outrage in the books that followed it. Nor are we apt, since Stuart Gilbert's monumental exegesis, to overlook the analogical structures or complain about its formlessness. On the other hand we have perhaps bent over too far in the direction of tolerance, losing both fun and mystery in the process. It is probably inevitable that each new generation of Joyceans will dig deeper in the text for its thrills, or, reacting as much to critics as to the book itself, speak of *Ulysses* as excessively controlled and cold, or discover unplanned incoherence. We come to *Ulysses* armed with the expectations it made possible and steeled in the school of Freud, Marx, Nietzsche, Frazer, Bergson, Einstein, to say nothing of their followers and rivals, or of Marshall McLuhan, Norman O. Brown, Norbert Wiener, Herbert Marcuse, Claude Lévi-Strauss, and Jacques Derrida. Yet, though some critics insist that Joyce's moral vision is impossibly dated, *Ulysses* is still very modern. Born out of the loss of firm faith in either sanctity, order, or progress, it is not a moral tract but rather a gigantic and perhaps even heroic effort to give esthetic order to the shellbits of our "Humptydump world" immersed in the "nightmare" of history.

The Road to Ithaca

Though he wrote neither a *roman fleuve* nor any two works in the same mode and though any one of his books may be read and en-

joyed separately, Joyce's novels and stories form a complex whole
and a comprehensive sequence. Reading them in the order of their
composition, we acquire skills and an awareness to correspond in a
measure to the artist's own developing and expanding vision
which was pushed inevitably toward the communal nightmare of
Finnegans Wake. (It is characteristic of Joyce that his first prepara-
tions for his last book were made under headings drawn systematically from each of his previous works.) Details, characters,
events, effects, and techniques from one work carry over into the
next much as the image or event occurring in one chapter will turn
up in later episodes as a symbol or an echo. Like the thrifty house-
wife, Joyce used the stock and ingredients from yesterday's soup to
flavor today's casserole. Accordingly, Tom Kernan, "that
drunken little barrelly man that bit his tongue off falling down the
mens WC drunk" (773) in "Grace," bumbles on as one of
Bloom's foils; and the sticks and birds used to such effect in the
Portrait are given fresh life in *Ulysses* and extended even into the
Wake. Since Joyce learned through writing, the technical break-
though of one book becomes a staple in the next. We cannot begin
our descriptive treatment of *Ulysses* without considering briefly the
works that it complements and continues.

The autobiographical essay "A Portrait of the Artist" suddenly
converted Joyce from aspiring playwright, poet, and critic into a
writer of prose fiction. Previously, he had written nothing closer to
serious fiction from a juvenile piece for *Titbits* (68–69), a collection
of sentimental sketches called *Silhouettes* which Richard Ellmann
describes as "avant-garde writing of the school of General
Booth,"[12] and of course those delicate records of revealing
moments Joyce called "epiphanies."[13] The "Portrait" essay represented a fresh departure. Written in a mannered, elliptical style
that recalls Walter Pater, J. K. Huysmans, and the poetic extravagance of Gabriele D'Annunzio, it is full of ironical jabs at his own
developing person, and larded with bits of his aesthetic and philo-
sophical asides. Stimulated, perhaps by the tone of Eglinton's refusal, Joyce abandoned this style when he started writing *Stephen
Hero*, a rather conventional novel of education despite its uncon-
ventional approach to a hero, at once admirable and fallible,
whose life was so closely patterned after the author's that Joyce
could affix dates to the chapters in his outline. (He planned to take

Stephen Dedalus from birth through Paris exile and return.) Seen in relation to *A Portrait*, the parts of *Stephen Hero* that have survived help illustrate the extent to which Joyce's command of his means had increased between 1904 and 1907. Here is a competent, even a polished narrative, which sets its protagonist in a clearly delineated ambience and treats him with respect from an ironic remove. There is nothing in this partial account of the university years which would have astonished readers of the time, though we may suppose that some of the missing sections contained graphic accounts of Stephen Dedalus' religious and sexual experience.

Joyce began writing *Dubliners* when George Russell, impressed by the bits of *Stephen Hero* he had read, suggested he write a story for his *Irish Homestead:* something "simple, rural, live-making, pathos [pathetic]."[14] Joyce quickly produced "The Sisters," a first person narrative which conveys through circumstantial details the reactions of a young boy to the illness and death of a paralyzed and demented old priest. The boy's essential ignorance, faithfully preserved in his past tense narrative, puts the burden of understanding on the reader, who is engaged by an intriguing blend of drama and mystery. Though Joyce did not then know it, this tale, signed with the name Stephen Daedalus, rendered the manner if not the conception of *Stephen Hero* obsolete as of the summer of 1904. The stories that followed, written in what Joyce called a style of scrupulous meanness and designed to expose to Dublin its own torpor, are a cross between satire and social criticism. Each tale is a vignette covering some aspect of the city's life, deftly pointing up a moral failure which the reader must extricate from the closely woven texture of the understated circumstances. The shorter form enabled Joyce to refine his techniques, to evolve among other things a powerful third person narrator capable of adjusting his voice to the character and circumstances and of conveying through calibrated indirection a wealth of implications which the simple surface belies. It was probably the writing of the last and most accomplished tale, "The Dead" (1907), that caused Joyce to scrap the novel. Here he had produced in his most objective voice a multi-personal situation focussed by a flash of recognition, a device he was to modify for the *Portrait.*

Nevertheless, when he decided to rename his novel *A Portrait of the Artist as a Young Man,* Joyce symbolically returned to his original conception, long since lost in the sprawling narrative of *Stephen Hero.* Ruthlessly cutting and doubtless altering the tone and perspective of the sections which now constitute chapters 1 through 3, he projected a five chapter format which would eventually suggest what he had called, in language that echoed his aesthetic theory, the "individuating rhythm" of Stephen's character, "the first or formal relation of [its] parts."[15] The result was something startling and fresh, a new wave of the tide which Joyce had described in 1901 as advancing "from Flaubert through Jakobsen [*sic;* Jens Peter Jacobsen, the Danish author of *Niels Lyhne*] to D'Annunzio."[16] Eliminating everything which did not contribute directly to the development of Stephen's "soul," whose symbolic release at the end of chapter 5 constitutes a second birth, Joyce sacrificed both transitions and the Dublin and home ambience. The *Portrait* records in interlocking prose vignettes the immediate impact and the underlying pattern of experiences that at once dictated and signaled its hero's growth. The new narrator, ostensibly the objective recorder of Stephen's awareness, is versatile and daring. Not only does he alter the style of each chapter to suggest a similar alteration in Stephen's nature, he also varies his tactics within a chapter. Stephen's first Christmas dinner is rendered as a modified Dickensian narrative that seems to open a window out into the world from his constricted consciousness. His religious crisis is interspersed with a literally transcribed series of sermons on last things, which dominates the pivotal third chapter. The book ends on a note as startling as the record of infant sensations with which it opens: Stephen's diary entries, recorded without comment in their pristine incoherence, signal his coming of age and engage us more immediately than ever in his aspirations while defining his triumph as a romantic illusion.

Already in *Dubliners* Joyce began tentatively introducing suggestive analogies for his protagonists and action. In the *Portrait,* where his goal was to create an individual who could serve as an ironic but not unworthy prototype of youthful heroism, he was far more systematic. He established, for example, a recognizable though veiled parallel with the Daedalus and Icarus myth which is expressed not only in terms of Stephen's awareness of his strange name and its connotations, but also through premonitory images. Carefully shaded allusions to birds (at first threatening and then gradually glorious and auspicious) or to figurative labyrinths (dark, narrow streets, hands forming a trap, rivulets meandering across a beach, nets) reflect upon and parallel both the development of Stephen's mind and his changing relationship to the Irish forces shaping him. Such images contribute to parallels that foreshadow the more systematic and numerous though not necessarily less subtle analogies which distract so many readers of *Ulysses* for whom the *Odyssey* parallel is a byword. They must be seen not only as part of the controlling and unifying mechanism but also as a commentary on the hero that is not entirely negative though it is certainly ironic.

While the evolution of the chapter styles in the *Portrait* chronicles a parallel development in Stephen's awareness and powers, the deliberately but subtly redundant chapter developments supported by the measured use of significant imagery relate that development of the "curve" of his identity seen as a "fluid succession of presents . . . of which [the] actual present is a phase only."[17] The typical chapter begins with a sentiment of impotence more than borne out by the disillusionments that follow and concludes on a note of new-found power which determines the direction of the next section. Such, Joyce implies, is the pattern of Stephen's life, and accordingly, he wrote *Ulysses* as the sixth chapter of that life, artfully withholding the conclusion.

All of this and much more is important to the reader of *Ulysses,* in which Joyce builds on his technical discoveries and in a sense reverses the perspective of the *Portrait,* presenting the individual in terms of the society upon which he reflects and in which he will find his own image. Also significant, of course, is a decision Joyce probably made between 1909 and 1912, to cut off Stephen's development at the moment of his first flight and to combine the next stage of his development with the adventures of Mr. Hunter-Bloom, whose day ends with his irrevocable awareness of his wife's adultery. In this way he drew on an already established counter rhythm, that of Stephen's awareness and of his aspiring youth to complicate and give value to his portrait of the Dublin everyman.

II

Dublin, June 16, 1904

Apprehending the Text

It is convenient to say that *Ulysses* is about a day in Dublin, a day that has become as famous as many historically more significant dates. Under the appearance of exhaustiveness, the book manages to present those details which reveal most tellingly the quality of that day. The illusion of completeness is most strongly conveyed in the experiences and reactions of a Dublin everyman-noman, Leopold Bloom, who is perhaps the most particularized character in all literature but who is also, and consequently, among the most generalized. Cast adrift by the accident of his wife's pending infidelity, but an habitual stranger in the land of his birth, he observes the world with exceptional clarity in spite of his inability to see or assert himself as distinct from it. To this indiscriminate but objective consciousness, Joyce added the selective, subjective, shaping consciousness of Stephen Dedalus, who experiences metaphysical confusion and struggles to establish for himself workable goals and a sense of his identity within a world he is unable to accept, unwilling to apprehend. *Ulysses,* like its principal models (*The Odyssey, The Divine Comedy, Hamlet,* and *Faust*), depicts a man's world, a world of ideas, objects, and actions, but woman provides a background and a focus for male activity. As in *Exiles* and *Finnegans Wake,* a woman has the last word, filling the space of the novel with unfettered musings welling up from secret sources of strength and turning on the nature of maleness which she subsumes.

Generically, there can be no doubt that *Ulysses* is a piece of prose

19

fiction in the novelistic tradition. But that tradition is notoriously heterogeneous, and Joyce's novel is remarkably innovative. The point is not that we should recognize in the brilliant synthesis a new mode or a fresh generic heading but rather that we should understand those qualities that set it apart so that we may better appreciate what it is on its own terms. Joyce has written an omnibook (or at least he has tried to write one and such an attempt is an heroic sort of folly), a book that responds to most of our tags but corresponds to none. Putting his playful intellect to work on a new sort of literary problem—how to convey in its integrity the modern predicament without defining man out of history—he has come up with startling and delightfully fresh literary solutions. It is tempting to play Joyce's own game and coin an absurd term like Stephen's "theolologicophilolological" (205) or Lynch's "Pornosophical philotheology" (432) to describe his accomplishment. But such comical designations, suggesting as they do a hash or an Irish stew (another of Joyce's terms), do more justice to the confused thought of a Stephen Dedalus than to the novel in which he appears. In *Ulysses* many separate voices contribute to a unified and coherent second creation, and we can trace paths through the labyrinth without losing the dramatic narrative they must serve. At any moment the dominant mode (say the farcical in "Circe" or "Cyclops" or the rhetorical in "Aeolus" or the comical in "Calypso") will derive support from other seemingly antagonistic modes. Frequently, what appear to be abrupt changes are the legitimate fruit of careful modulation and far from inexplicable. While the fates of Stephen, Bloom, and Molly, to say nothing of the other Dubliners, are inextricably entwined, all are ultimately and emphatically distinct. *Ulysses* may well be an *Eintopf,* but if so, it is one of those engrossing Chinese soups, each of whose many ingredients remains magically distinct in a savory broth to which each contributes something indefinable.

Joyce's title and his systematic use of the homeric and other analogies point up a much-discussed aspect of *Ulysses,* its status as a modern prose epic, or a mock epic novel. Surely his ambitions were epic. That is, he chose to evoke through a single coherent circumstance and with encyclopedic intensity the quality and spirit of a nation and an epoch. He chose as his protagonists exemplary figures (or rather figures that can be thought of as exemplary) and yet tried to convey the gravity of their personal dilemmas. At the same time he seemingly reversed the prime quality of most epics, choosing to depict antiheroes, apparent failures, preferring the trivial circumstance to the momentous, the irreverent attitude to the reverent, dispensing with harmonious and elevated style and tone. The scope of his narrative is another matter. Homer manages to confine his action to a few days while dealing with a ten-year period. The events he describes take us all over the known world *and* to Hades and Olympus. Dante's internal pilgrimage with its four levels of interpretation takes him in jig time through the earth and into the heavens before depositing him on his own doorstep, and depicts him as human and fallible while subjecting him to visions ranging from absolute debasement to absolute elevation. Goethe's *Faust* spans heaven and hell, telescopes history, takes its learned hero through every section of his society in the company of a diabolic clown who may be thought of as an aspect of his own character. Each of these is in some sense a serious epic, a titanic vision in contrast to which Joyce's simple plot and mundane setting is dwarfed unless we take into consideration the detailed analogies, the complexity of his vision, the range of his styles, and the fact that he explores as no one else the inner and outer aspects of the human predicament. Ultimately, *Ulysses* stands on the epic scale somewhere between the serious works Joyce pretends to mimic and the comic and mock epics which it resembles in so many of its details: works like Petronius' *Satyricon* with its clownish protagonists, its stylistic verve, and its persistent outrage; Rabelais's *Gargantua and Pantagruel,* which inflates the commonplace and delights in the absurd; and Sterne's *Tristram Shandy,* which turns style and stylist into clownish personae and spoofs the reader's expectations. There is always a serious undertone to Joyce's fun and a comic tinge to his seriousness. He has managed to show the extraordinary as a quality of the ordinary. By altering comic practice, he has made an exemplary norm of the exception and the failure. Systematically working against conventions too numerous to list, he has behaved in a most conventional manner and written a book that is totally rational and coherent, balanced and harmonious.

Though the characterization or rather the exposure of character through action and reaction is very important in *Ulysses,* plot and engrossing action become almost vestigial. In fact they frequently function as they do in Virginia Woolf's *The Waves,* where all of the physical action takes place, so to speak, off stage and we are given only its reflection in the distorting mirror of the characters' minds. Or again, as in a symbolist poem, the objective universe of *Ulysses* is frequently glimpsed *through the medium* (i.e., the style itself) and *in terms* of it rather than *in* the novel, and our pleasure is drawn from the process of apprehending what happens, the meaning of what happens, and the expression which is in itself an event. In a stream of consciousness passage, for example, we are more interested in the effect of the particulars on the character than in the detail itself until we realize that it too has its functions which ultimately, though often indirectly, add to our sense of action and meaning. Joyce gives us details and actions in solution and obliges us to sort out the givens, reconstitute first the moment, then its effect and significance. Then perhaps, we may return to the detail for new treasures. Under these circumstances plot and even the simplest particulars of the action become rewards for diligent reading, the donkey's carrot which many conscientious readers never quite consume.

This need not invalidate the usual questions, the whats and whys of motivation, but it does make them harder to phrase and answer and it puts such questions elsewhere, if not lower, on the scale of values. As if to emphasize this, Joyce permits apparently trivial details to operate as symbols, forming curious clusters. The motto of a potted meat company, the missing letter on Bloom's hat band ("ha"), the letter left out of his name in the newspaper account of Dignam's funeral ("Boom"), and the lagging sandwich-man in the procession spelling out "H.E.L.Y.'S." all contribute to our sense of the incompleteness and inadequacy of Bloom's position. Or again, in a lighter and lower vein, we have two female activities constituting the poles of the book or rather opening and closing the circle of its action. In the first chapter Stephen imagines the old milk woman whom he associates with Ireland, "Crouching by a patient cow at daybreak . . . a witch on her toadstool" (13). It is almost 3 a.m. when a lusty Molly Bloom rises from the jingling bed to squat on an "orange-keyed chamberpot" (64, 770), which according to Bloom "has only one handle" (547). Here we find a typical symbolic pleasantry and as neat a symbolic cluster as any in the book. These two female images may suggest life and death interchangeably. The pot is incomplete, recalling not only the inadequacy of the Blooms' relationship but also the image of the "one-handled adulterer," Lord Nelson, whose monument is the site of a wasteland fertility ceremony imagined by Stephen. Bloom, who has left his housekey, the symbol of his functions and of home rule, in Molly's room, spends his day searching for a way to return. Stephen, who must cut loose if he is to actualize his potential, has left behind the impossibly heavy key to the tower which his friend Mulligan calls the omphalos (see the navel of the world and the cord connecting us to the primal and the temporal womb). Orange is the color of the Protestant Lodges of the North and the Protestant establishment controls Catholic Ireland. The simple and useful object on which Molly squats is then also an irreverent symbol for the keys, the omphalos-tower, Home Rule for Ireland, and the female potential.

Joyce handles such details with studied negligence, permits them to play like lights on the surface of the action. He is even more casual with the sort of vital statistics another novelist might deliver into our hands in his first chapter. We must keep our eyes open if we are to find Bloom's age, his marriage date, the jobs he has held and lost. We must piece together Stephen's reasons for leaving his father's house, to say nothing of why he goes to the National Library in "Scylla and Charybdis" or to Horne's lying-in hospital in "Oxen of the Sun." Such details and a host of others are suppressed or glossed over or dropped casually into the flood of facts where they surprise and delight a reader almost as much as the solution to a good mystery. Since nothing of obvious moment happens during the day of *Ulysses* and no one of exceptional stature walks the streets of Dublin, it is a tribute to Joyce's art that we are intrigued when we find that while Stephen *walks* in solipsistic anguish on the beach in "Proteus," the all-too-relaxed Bloom *sits* on the beach in "Nausikaa." Or again it matters to us as it does to Bloom that Molly has probably been faithful during Bloom's ten years of relative abstinence and that Boylan is probably her first lover, though we have been encouraged up to the last chapter to see her as a monumental whore.[1] For the justification on the naturalistic level of Stephen's hallucinated behavior in "Proteus" and elsewhere, we should know that he needs and lacks glasses, a fact mentioned only in "Circe" where Stephen, who is having trouble lighting his cigarette, remarks, "Must get glasses. Broke them yesterday" (560).[2] Such facts alter our conception of characters, others simply increase our enjoyment of the moment, but inevitably, as a consequence of Joyce's method, we will miss something, for there is too much here to meet the eye and tease the intellect.

Stephen in the Plot*

Since, even on the "realistic" level, *Ulysses* suggests multiple readings, any single account of the plot is bound to include a degree of interpretation that will limit its value by excluding other readings and fixing what is otherwise a fluid circumstance. The following brief summary is my "version" of what happens to the questers during their eighteen hours of equal-opposite peregrination through the phenomenal world toward the silent stasis of the womb and the turbulence of rebirth.

Poor, bedraggled, and still unfledged, Stephen has returned to Ireland from Paris, where he read much but wrote little. A grounded hawk among wild geese, he learned bitterness, disillusionment, and some French, and lost nothing by returning to watch his mother die of cancer. He is a gloomy figure, in mourning as much for his own intransigence at not having prayed at his mother's bedside as for the love he feels unable to replace. Having abandoned a home ill-served by his profligate and quarrelsome father, he has returned to his university environment, renting a Martello tower[3] in which for ten days he has lived riotously with Buck Mulligan. (With encyclopedic thoroughness Joyce has here begun to suggest ironic parallels, seeing, for example, in the Irish literary renaissance confused echoes of the ferment of Renaissance England, the sparkle of the eighteenth century and the brilliance of fifth century Athens. Among other things, he may be playing on

---

* For a more schematic rendering of the chapter development, see appendix I.

the friendship between the young provincial Shakespeare and his cultivated friend Ben Jonson, a relationship that must have tickled his fancy.) A clever poetaster who hobnobs as an equal with the lights, Buck is Stephen's discoverer and initiator, as well as the successor to the dour Cranly of the *Portrait*. Is is clear that, like Buck, and despite himself, Stephen still shares with the Irish intelligentsia and the mystics an addiction to the *fin de siècle* spirit, as witness the quatrain he writes on the beach during "Proteus" and quotes in "Aeolus." It is also fairly clear that he feels instinctively dissatisfied with that moment's fading bloom and trapped by an allegiance which has not fertilized his muse. Stephen is still the "artist as a young man," a fact which no amount of cynicism can dispel. To understand the nature of his dilemma we need only read in the poetry of Baudelaire, Mallarmé, and Verlaine, the theatre of Maeterlinck, or the derivative poems of Swinburne and Wilde, both of whom Mulligan admires. Such writers, though brilliant, are dangerously accessible to the imitators, the mockers, and the faddists, who seem suddenly to have replaced the philistines as Stephen's foils in Dublin.

Apart from its symbolic echoes, as womb, phallus or oracular omphalos, temple, castle or cell, the tower is an aesthetic image of romantic isolation, a cliché from the past by which Stephen feels trapped. His terrified reaction to Haines's black panther nightmare of the previous night, blending with his own dream-vision of his dead mother as a ghostly presence, is only the immediate source of his statement to Mr. Deasy: "History . . . is a nightmare from which I am trying to awake" (34). Caught, like Goethe's Faust, in a past both distant and recent, he desires to wake into his own present. We may feel that he has not really moved very far since he broke with adolescence on the beach in chapter 4 of the *Portrait,* where the lovely Pre-Raphaelite image of the bird-girl threw "open before him in an instant of ecstasy the gates of all the ways of error and glory."[4] But the fact that he seems now to crave another such revelation, one capable of setting him free once more, need not confuse us. He has come a long way along the "curve" of his identity and is perhaps ready for a different sort of initiation by another sort of angel.

At 8 a.m. in the Martello tower Stephen climbs the staircase to speak to the shaving, gesticulating, ebullient, protean Mulligan about Haines's nightmare and indirectly about his own concern with pride and guilt. After brooding on his outrage and shame, he joins the others below where Mulligan, who has fixed breakfast, makes mocking allusions to him as a servant, allusions Stephen takes to his symbol-loving heart and nourishes along with other slights that darken his day. It is not hard to understand Stephen's resentment at being obliged to shine for the greater glory of a man who repeatedly outshines him, though, given his enormous lucidity, it may be hard to appreciate the self-destructive urge and the frustrations that have led him to confide in Buck and the inertia that keeps them together. We may be sure that there is some mystic crux here and that Stephen, ever eager like the German mystic Jakob Böhme to read the "signatures of all things" (37), sees Mulligan as a necessary evil, a needed scourge and goad. "Offend me still. Speak on" (218), he mutters several hours later as they leave the National Library together. It follows then that the old milkwoman who favors the bantering Mulligan is an allegory of Ireland, the Shan Van Vocht, or "poor old woman," bowing to false values. Mulligan washing, dressing, undressing, and diving into the "forty foot hole" (or men's swimming area) is for the poorly clad hydrophobe an allegory of guilt and usurpation. Even more painful for one who has lived through his own moment of soaring daedalian aspirations on the beach in the *Portrait* is the sight of Mulligan's fluttering birdhands as he dives, a graceful but comic Icarus, into the water Stephen fears. Still, at Buck's insistence, he leaves behind the tower key and twopence for beer and promises to meet him at a pub called The Ship where they will begin spending Stephen's salary and he will elaborate his Shakespeare theory for the well-heeled Haines. Stephen has already decided not to return to the tower: "I will not sleep here tonight. Home also I cannot go." But it should not be assumed that he has really made up his mind.

There are large gaps in the action of "Telemachus," despite the meticulous attention to details. For one thing, while Stephen thinks, the action continues. What Stephen overlooks, we too miss. Again, though we watch Mulligan shave, eat, cavort, dress, and finally bathe, we see Stephen performing only minimal ac tions. We may well feel that his detachment on this level approaches morbid asceticism, an impression Joyce supports throughout the book, permitting us to see him take little more than liquid refreshment and emphasizing his utter disregard for things of this world, his joyless prodigality. Like Faust, he is an incomplete man, one who has cultivated his spirit at the expense of his flesh and who is now embittered by the quality of his rewards. Perhaps the circumstance of his mother's death, perhaps the failure of his art, perhaps the cool reception given him by the Dublin literary establishment, perhaps his sense of being dragged back into the Irish quagmire he thought he had flown above, perhaps all of these things together have confused and paralyzed him. At any rate (and in this he resembles an Irish Hamlet), he fills those parts of his day we witness with activities designed to disguise his sense of futility but drawing him inevitably closer to a moment of decision.

The hours between 9 and 11 ("Nestor"), of which we see only a fraction, are spent in Deasy's school. There, more engaged by his own historical consciousness than by their evident lack of interest, Stephen catechizes Protestant boys in their lessons and vainly tries to amuse them with a pointless riddle. An inept teacher or "gentleman usher" reenacting his own boyhood and schooling at Clongowes Wood, he feels drawn only to a class weakling. Contemplating this child he sees his own enslavement to a dim personal past and unconsciously predicts the necessary chaos of "Circe": "Secrets, silent, stony sit in the dark palaces of both our hearts: secrets weary of their tyranny: tyrants willing to be dethroned" (28). It is Thursday, a halfday, and as the boys rush out to play (another echo from his past), Stephen switches roles to become the reluctant pupil of the crusty and opinionated and yet fatherly Mr. Deasy. He listens uneasily to anti-Fenian, anti-Semitic and anti-feminist diatribes and receives, with his salary, lectures on history and economy, and a letter on hoof and mouth disease which he promises to deliver to his journalist acquaintances. Torn as he is between his roles (boy-man, Catholic-renegade, Irishman-exile, etc.), Stephen's attitude toward Deasy is too complex to be characterized as "unforced respect."[5] The old man is painfully right in several of his judgments, especially when he states, from a contrary position, opinions that parallel Stephen's own (see chapter 5 of the *Portrait*) about the Irish and their heroes, and when he reminds Stephen of his improvidence and suggests that he has no vocation for teaching. He is both a wise Nestor and a prattling old man, a Polonius, unable to understand that Hamlet-Stephen "has reasons." Their spirited quarrel over the vices of the Jews, the only point which Stephen deigns to dispute, must be seen in the perspective of the "Scylla and Charybdis" discussion of Shakespeare's Semitism and Stephen's nocturnal visit with the unacquisitive commercial failure, Bloom.

Sometime, perhaps between 11 and 12 ("Proteus"), rather than keep his appointment at The Ship, Stephen sends Mulligan a telegram which suggestively paraphrases George Meredith: *"The sentimentalist is he who would enjoy without incurring the immense debtorship for a thing done"* (199). We do not see him sending the telegram or approaching the beach at Sandymount, but we accompany him as he wanders, uncertain of his immediate goal but at last alone with his myriad thoughts. During this dense chapter he makes a decision or two by default (not to walk out into the sea, not to visit Uncle Richie) and performs two significant actions: he tears off some paper from Deasy's letter to write the quatrain inspired by a pair of cockle-pickers; towards the end of the chapter he sits on a rock and indulges in what appears to be characteristically cerebral autoerotic behavior.[6] But mainly the time is taken up by random musings inspired by the sea, the beach, and his own dim sight: an inner soliloquy astonishingly rich in verbal events and allusions but consistently solipsistic. Desperately limited by his nature and nurture, he is a pathetic and cynical shadow of his naïvely hopeful younger self:

> Reading two pages apiece of seven books every night, eh? I was young. You bowed to yourself in the mirror, stepping forward to applause earnestly, striking face. Hurray for the Goddamned idiot! Hray! No-one saw; tell no-one. Books you were going to write with letters for titles. (40)

In "Aeolus," Stephen's and Bloom's paths first cross as Stephen delivers a copy of Deasy's letter to the barmy editor of the *Evening Telegraph,* a chore we may suspect Stephen accepted partly to kill time, partly to please the old man whom he grudgingly admires. Perhaps too he sees journalism as a way out of his impasse and a source of funds; if so his reaction to Miles Crawford's vague offer of a commission (to write a satirical piece!?) is equivocal. At their best the rhetoricians have nothing to offer him. The lover of language is not apt to be delighted by words of praise uttered by wasted men for the wasted words of Irish public speakers. In stark contrast we have his own offering, the original, inconclusive "Parable of the Plums" inspired by his epiphany of two "midwives" crossing the beach in "Proteus." The "Parable," recited as Stephen leads the mob to a pub, is received generously but, like the riddle in "Nestor," with incomprehension.

His visit to the pub has left Stephen light-headed and courageous enough to beard the pseudonymous pundits at the National Library ("Scylla and Charybdis"): John Eglinton (Magee), and AE (George Russell). He may have come to the librarian's office in order to put Deasy's letter in AE's hands,[7] but he may also have come in quest of Haines who speaks of the library in "Telemachus." As usual, he is torn between conflicting emotions and aspirations. Despite the ironical asides, he respects Eglinton's Aristotelian rigor and craves both his attention and his approval. As for AE, Stephen's feigned indifference ("Stephen looked down on the wide headless caubeen, hung on his ashplanthandle over his knee" [192].)[8] underscores his resentment at being excluded from the list of Irish literary hopefuls whom, ironically, he neither envies nor respects. Amidst the frustrating entrances and departures in this public place, he expounds his Shakespeare theory to a worthy but unsympathetic and easily distracted audience, attempting to demonstrate to them and to himself that he is both an intellectual and a critic. Halfway through the argument, though not before the departure of AE, Mulligan bursts in to assert his dominion over his friend. His ribald wit provides the comic relief that dampens Stephen's spirits and reaffirms the fact that "Kinch" is miscast as a public performer in an Ireland where the clown and bone setter is valued above the priest of art. If he has come to the library hoping to sell the Shakespeare theory to Magee's magazine, *Dana*, Stephen is disappointed, but we have the sense that he is beyond hope and that each of his acts is a act of desperation designed to convince him of his own failure and leading towards the violence or suicide hinted at in "Proteus" and "Wandering Rocks."

Stephen's Shakespeare argument may be seen as an intellectual and critical exercise in the then popular biographical vein,[9] a substitute for true creative activity, a set piece. But on this day Stephen has little besides his ready wit to second his claim to public attention and help pay his debts. The difference between the famous esthetics conversation with Lynch in chapter 5 of the *Portrait* and this tense and tendentious argument is another symptom of Stephen's fall. In the *Portrait* a relaxed and self-confident Stephen deliberately chose in the reptilian mocker, Lynch, the peer least likely to approve or understand his theory. Here, unsure of himself in the presence of experts, Stephen is less systematic, more brilliant, and more vulnerable. Fleshing out his Aristotle ("Unsheathe your dagger definitions [186].) with the aid of his Jesuit training ("Composition of place. Ignatius Loyola, make haste to help me!" [188] and relying of all things on the techniques used in the hell-fire retreat sermons of the third chapter in the *Portrait,* he is engaged both in a creative activity, that is, in making Shakespeare's milieu and predicament vital in the halls of dead learning, and in a personal and pseudo-religious meditation on the trinitarian nature of the artist's relationship to his person and his creation. Tension is generated not only by his sense of failure but also by the emotional conflicts that have sterilized him and permitted others to usurp his laurels.

At about 3 p.m. ("Wandering Rocks") Stephen leaves the library with Mulligan, whom Simon Dedalus has roundly cursed in "Hades" as "a contaminated bloody doubledyed ruffian . . . His name stinks all over Dublin" (88).[10] When they separate, Mulligan goes to meet Haines for tea. As one of the rocks amid which the Lord Lieutenant's cavalcade weaves its way toward the opening of the Mirus Bazaar, Stephen is next seen chatting in Italian with Almidano Artifoni, who urges him to reconsider a decision to give up a possible singing career. Later, he surprises his sister Dilly buying a used French text and sees in her mute admiration a reminder of his own failure. This, plus the view we have of the Dedalus family life, the grinding poverty and the scrounging for crusts, justifies Stephen's melodramatic fear of being submerged by their ruin: "She is drowning. Agenbite. Save her . . . She will drown me with her, eyes and hair" (243).

We can assume the various accounts of Stephen's finances (see for example pages 556–59) that he spends the rest of his day wandering aimlessly and not entirely alone. It is about 10 p.m. when Bloom finds him at the Holles Street hospital ("Oxen of the Sun") where Mulligan has promised to meet him after the literary evening at George Moore's house. Brilliantly drunk, Stephen is carousing with medical johnnies and professional parasites, trading puerile quips, elaborating clever conceits, and blaspheming, while, upstairs, Mrs. Mina Purefoy is painfully and belatedly delivered of her nth infant. The group is joined by Bloom and later by Mulligan, who as usual dominates the talk and dampens Stephen's spirits. After the birth, the noisy group spills out into the street, recently watered by a frightening and perhaps fructifying thundershower, for a final drink at Burke's pub where Stephen, as usual, treats.

In the drunken confusion after pub-closing at 11 p.m., Mulligan and Haines give Stephen the slip (perhaps after an argument):

> Where's the buck and Namby Amby? Skunked? Leg bail. Aweel, ye maun e'en gang yer gates. Checkmate. King to tower. Kind Kristyann will yu help, young man hoose frend tuk bungalo kee to find plais whear to lay crown off his hed 2 night. (427)

Stephen, who has silently lusted all day, takes Lynch to Bella Cohen's brothel only to learn that his favorite whore, the clergyman's daughter Georgina Johnson, has married a traveling man (560). Through most of "Circe," while Bloom watches protectively, he prates scholarly gibberish and barely comprehensible theory, hallucinating mildly while Lynch plays sardonic whetstone. Finally, he breaks out of his torpor into a wild dance which occasions the gruesome but saccharine vision of his dead mother, emblem of the force that has brought him back from Paris and now refuses to release him from Ireland, absolve him of his guilt, and remove his fear of death. Stephen hysterically rejects her melodramatic claims and accusations and then dispels her image by at-

tacking with his ashplant the mauve lampshade. Dashing out into
the street, leaving the vigilant and fatherly Bloom to settle with the
whoremistress, he inadvertently offends a British tommy in the
course of an absurd altercation during which he hallucinates about
England in the shape of Edward VII and Ireland as Old Gummy
Granny, both of whom he loudly but incoherently rejects. In the
end he is knocked unconscious by a clumsy blow from the uncomprehending private but protected by Bloom who revives him and
then encourages him "in orthodox Samaritan fashion" (613)
("Eumaeus") to come along for refreshments.

It is after 1 a.m. when they stop at the cabman's shelter sup-
posedly run by an ex-Invincible and drink undrinkable coffee
while a garrulous sailor spins drunken lies. This is the moment
Joyce has so carefully prepared us for, when his Ulysses discloses
his identity to his Telemachus. We watch expectantly for the
marks of recognition, but Stephen, still groggy from the blow and
perhaps still a bit drunk, seems more willing to speak to a sponging
Corley, whom he mockingly sends to Deasy after his own job, than
to Bloom. In "Nestor," he defended the Jews in the abstract for
qualities he later discovered in his Shakespeare. Here he finds in
Bloom not the mysterious homeless wanderer but a wandering
commonplace on his way home. If the two make contact, it is on
the level of music and the songs Stephen sings as they walk arm in
arm toward number 7 Eccles Street. After all, Stephen has discovered in Bloom a degree of strangeness:

> Accordingly he passed his left arm in Stephen's right and
> led him on accordingly.
> —Yes, Stephen said uncertainly, because he thought he
> felt a strange kind of flesh of a different man approach him,
> sinewless and wobbly and all that. (660)

We are reminded of earlier references to Cranly's and Mulligan's
arms and are subtly aware that Stephen's sensation might signal a
real change in his condition after the rite of passage into the night
that is "Circe." However, though Stephen implicitly wishes to be
initiated, like Shakespeare, by an older woman (see "Scylla and
Charybdis" [191]: "And my turn? When?") and though he has
probably overheard Dixon's remarks about Molly's charms and

availability (425.16–24), he does not seem attracted by the idea of giving Molly lessons on an exchange basis. Having rejected the claims of one mother, he is doubtless unwilling to take on another.

In "Ithaca," from which emotions and reactions are systematically excluded, he drinks Epp's cocoa, exchanges a few opinions, and politely refuses an invitation to spend the night. But before the "centrifugal departer" leaves the "centripetal remainer," in a ceremonial gesture common to members of the canine species, the two men mingle their waters in the already watered wasteland garden. Stephen, whose destination is unspecified, has made no great effort to endear himself to Bloom. Rather, he has been gently if acidly humorous and even playful enough to sing an anti-Semitic song to his embarrassed but tolerant semi-Semitic host. There will be no sequel to this visit.

The Wandering Bloom

If, from the point of view of Joyce's readers, Stephen is prolonging an already established curve, his equal-opposite comes to us fresh and strange through that grand opening sentence of "Calypso": "Mr Leopold Bloom ate with relish the inner organs of beasts and fowls" (55). He is the very substance of the Old Testament smoke-eating "Jehovah, collector of prepuces" (201) though somewhat softened by the passage of the centuries. Bloom's day is a complete life: past, present, and probable future. Joyce builds him gradually through the memories and reactions of others as well as through his own memories and sensations, delightful as they are trivial, served warm with a seasoning of life and laced with laughter. Putting the facts together, we find that he is thirty-eight years old, the son of a Hungarian Jewish immigrant who changed his name from Virag and married an Irish woman. His recollection of Virag's suicide, combined with a sense of having abandoned or lost the traditions of his fathers, reflects in a lighter vein Stephen's distress over his mother's death and his gnawing "agenbite of inwit." He has married Molly Tweedy, the daughter of an Irish Sergeant Major stationed on Gibraltar and a Spanish Jewess of questionable morals. They have had a daughter, Milly, fifteen, now a photographer's assistant in the market town of Mullingar, and a son, Rudolph, named after his grandfather, but dead at eleven days, eleven years ago.

Intelligent, but untrained and only moderately gifted, Bloom is not a good provider. Having been a peddler of trinkets, a traveler for blotting paper, a clerk in a slaughter house, and, in hard times, a salesman for the "Royal Hungarian Lottery," he now makes a meager living canvassing for ads for the *Weekly Freeman*.[11] As Madame Marion Tweety, Molly helps support the family with her singing and is currently planning a tour with Blazes Boylan as her manager. Since the death of their son, which was traumatic for both of them, Bloom and Molly have had no normal sexual relations. Molly seems to have gone her own way. She is now beginning what appears to be her first affair with the "Worst man in Dublin" (92), as Bloom calls Boylan. Recently, instead of renewing normal relations, Bloom has advertised for a mistress. Under the pseudonym Henry Flower, he is now corresponding with a lovelorn typist, who signs herself Martha Clifford. He is, however, throughly monogamous. Molly was and is his great romance: the seduction on the Hill of Howth, like Shakespeare's seduction in a rye field, remains the sensual event of his life.

A diffident and abstemious man in convivial and bibulous Dublin, Bloom has many acquaintances but few friends. Though he may be a Mason[12] and hence may partake of a secular mysticism (see, by way of contrast, Stephen's esoteric preoccupations), he makes little of that association and less of his prior commitments to Protestantism and Catholicism, to say nothing of the Judaism into which he was born but apparently not initiated. Moderate in everything, except perhaps his secret lusts, he enters *Ulysses* as a thoroughly eclectic and vaguely sympathetic man in a city full of quirky individuals, a man who sips cautiously the cup of life, taking care not to swallow too many bubbles. Altogether, he is a worthy successor to the numerous nineteenth-century antiheroes and especially to Charles Bovary, whose miseries and joys are scamped in Flaubert's account of the philandering Emma.

Bloom's day begins with an 8 a.m. breakfast at 7 Eccles Street ("Calypso"), a very ordinary Dublin address and the former home of Joyce's friend Byrne, the "Cranly" of the *Portrait*. While Molly lies upstairs in old man Cohen's jingling bed which her husband believes that Tweedy brought back from Gibraltar, Bloom buys a breakfast kidney at the Jewish pork butcher's, serves her tea, and gets the mail which contains, along with a letter to him from Milly, a note to Molly from Boylan, who is coming to see her at 4:00 in the afternoon. This note and this knowledge keep Bloom away from home till 2 a.m. Unlike Stephen, who must decide whether or not to return to Mulligan and the tower, Bloom must decide when to return to Molly. After breakfast, he goes to the garden privy, where he reads and then wipes himself with a prize story in *Titbits,* an emblem of his literary ambitions. Like Stephen, but for this day only, Bloom is in mourning and keyless. Having changed his suit so that he can attend the funeral of little Paddy Dignam of the red nose, he inadvertently leaves his keys in Molly's room.

"Lotus Eaters" finds Bloom at 10 o'clock in another part of town on his way to the baths. His actions and reactions reflect the coming euphoria. As Henry Flower, he picks up and eventually reads a teasing letter with a flower enclosure from Martha Clifford. He tells the cadger, M'Coy, about his wife's tour and promises to sign him in at the funeral. He buys some soap for his bath and orders some lotion for Molly and inadvertently gives Bantam Lyons a tip on the horse Throwaway in the Gold Cup race. Finally, to kill time, he drops in to watch a mass with cool and comic objectivity.

At 11 o'clock ("Hades"), he joins the funeral party and crosses town to Glasnevin cemetery in a carriage with Simon Dedalus, Martin Cunningham, and John Power, for whom he is clearly an outsider. During the ride he sees Stephen on his way to the beach and points him out to a barely civil Simon, who turns the youth into an object of Bloom's fatherly concern. After the cemetery he tells one of Molly's rejected admirers, the pompous John Henry Menton, that he has a dint in his hat, only to be rudely ignored. This action parallels not only the behavior of Ajax' ghost toward Ulysses but also the gracious thankyou Bloom received years earlier when he picked up Parnell's hat.

Bloom turns up next at the drafty *Freeman* office ("Aeolus"), where he is negotiating the terms and layout for an ad for the House of Keyes. We see him only briefly and share few of his thoughts and words in this chapter, which is dominated by the journalistic grubs. Rushing back and forth, suffering minor indignities, and winning minor concessions from busy pressmen and the cantankerous editor, he is curtly rebuffed when he interrupts the pub-pilgrimage to ask for one final favor. All in all he cuts a figure of comic competence in a world of empty words and sham concerns: "Time someone thought about [easing the pains of childbirth]," thinks the ever-considerate canvasser reacting against the rhetoric, "instead of gassing about the what was it the pensive bosom of the silver effulgence. Flapdoodle to feed fools on" (161).[13]

In "Lestrygonians," between 1 and 2 p.m., Bloom's thoughts turn on food and disgust as he searches for a suitable place to eat. Rejecting Burton's Restaurant where the masticating horde turns his stomach, he settles on Davy Byrne's pub. There he finds a flea-bitten admirer in Nosey Flynn. Earlier he has met a former flame, Josie Powell Breen, married now to the dotty Denis, whose behavior gives us a foretaste of Bloom's moon-madness in "Circe." Unlike those who grudgingly applaud Stephen, Bloom's admirers are a curious lot, whose admiration springs from ignorance rather than understanding and whose presence and praise is an embarrassment to him and to us. After his snack, Bloom wanders toward the National Library, a keyless man in quest of copy for the Keyes ad. On his way he helps a blind stripling across the street, a gesture that foreshadows his meeting with the weak-eyed Stephen. Finally he dodges into the museum opposite the library to avoid meeting Boylan: "Straw hat in sunlight. Tan shoes. Turnedup trousers. It is. It is" (183).

During the Shakespeare argument in "Scylla and Charybdis," where Stephen sketches a Bloomlike bard, Bloom is part of the background. Only Mulligan, who has just seen him in the museum investigating the hinder parts of a Venus, notes his presence. Bloom's great moment comes when he sails out of the library between Buck and Stephen in an innocent parody of the mythical escape. We see him briefly in "Wandering Rocks" renting pornography for Molly. Neither he nor Stephen is included in the catalogue of watchers at the end of this chapter.

Shortly before 4 p.m. ("Sirens"), he drops in at the Ormond Hotel bar during a wary and curiously sensual pursuit of Boylan, whose visit to Molly shames and subconsciously pleases him. Sad and lonely, his head filled with thoughts of Molly, he lunches on liver and cider in the company of Stephen's uncle Richie Goulding and stealthily writes a note to Martha. For much of this time Bloom is orchestrated into the musical texture of "Sirens," where the foreground is occupied by flirtatious barmaids to whose charms he is generally deaf but into whose orbit are drawn brilliant performers (siren singers) like Simon Dedalus and Ben Dollard, the unfrocked priest Father Cowley, the sly cadging Lenehan, and of course dashing Blazes Boylan, who quickly departs in his hired cab but whose jingling progress we follow to his goal. True to his word in the *Exiles* notes, Joyce has made the seducer an insipid if flashy fancyman, a powerful but unworthy rival, as Molly's reactions in "Penelope" indicate. Boylan, the carefree conqueror, represents the world of trivial business deals, sporting life, pub talk, and casual alliances. He is appropriately seen in transit and conveniently dismissed to remain a presence only in the minds of other characters and a reproach to Bloom.

It is 5 o'clock ("Cyclops") when Bloom, keeping an appointment to help settle the affairs of Dignam's widow, stations himself in front of Barney Kiernan's pub. Here the focus is on the assorted drinkers gathered around a broken down "patriot" who calls himself "citizen" and glories in his and Ireland's past. Much against his wishes, Bloom is dragged into the group which knows him as a freemason and a Jew and suspects him of having won on Throwaway, a twenty-to-one bet at the Ascot Races (325). His failure to buy anything for the thirsty cadgers (or accept anything but a "knock-me-down cigar") combines with his oppressive reasonableness in this den of unreason or false reasoning to provoke an anti-Semitic eruption. Bloom's last gesture is a gallant defense of the Jews, among whom he numbers the son of an apostate (Mendelssohn), apostates (Marx and Spinoza), a gentile (Mercadante), and of course Jesus Christ. It prompts the irate and drunken citizen-cyclops to throw a biscuit tin in the direction of the departing cab in a scene that foreshadows Stephen's street brawl in "Circe."

For all the minutiae in *Ulysses,* and despite the completeness of Bloom's characterization, mercifully, much is left to our imaginations. We share his thoughtstream for only a handful of the day's hours and in relatively few chapters. Though he defecates and urinates before us, he shaves, dresses, and bathes offstage. We accompany him neither to Keyes's shop where he conducts business nor to Mrs. Dignam's house where he discusses insurance. Though the missing details may be tucked into his revery, there is little room for redundancy in a book where every gesture bears on character and theme. Mulligan's shaving, dressing, and bathing must suffice for Bloom as well. It is fitting then that, after two blank hours, Bloom appears on Sandymount Strand at 8 p.m. ("Nausikaa"). There he watches the flirtatious behavior of Gerty MacDowell, a coy virgin in her early twenties, nourished on lady's periodical literature. During Gerty's deliberately but archly seductive leg-swinging performance, Bloom is silent, the distant stranger of her sentimental dream. His own performance is reflected through her monologue by a sugary shock of pleasure and shame. In the second half of the chapter we shift our field and see the departing Gerty through Bloom's objective eyes as he straightens out his clothes and contemplates but rejects the idea of repeating the experience. The masturbation during the fireworks display for the Mirus Bazaar, a sunset ceremony (that follows the celebration of the Virgin in a neighboring church!), partially explains his abstinence in "Circe."

Having dozed off briefly on the beach, but still unwilling to risk an encounter with Boylan, Bloom goes to the Holles Street hospital ("Oxen of the Sun") to enquire about Mina Purefoy, who is still in childbirth. Dixon, the young intern who once dressed a bee sting for him, draws him into the anteroom. He sits there, uncomfortably abstemious, among the clever young sports, and there he sees the young student (Bannon) who is Milly's first boyfriend. Among the barflies at Kiernan's he was out of place but intellectually superior. Here, the unwitting or good-natured butt of witticisms and the victim of Mulligan's veiled hostility, he is in beyond his intellectual depth. Concerned over Stephen's drunken condition, he follows him to Burke's pub and then to nighttown.

What actually occurs to him in "Circe" is simple but muzzy for the reader who must attend not only to events but to illusions. Joyce involves us from the start in the hallucinated context, generating through his stage directions a dream landscape out of the and most degrading of his visions, being turned in his imagination into something approximating one of Circe's pigs. The grotesque, absurd, and obscene sequence concludes with the sound of a snapping trouser button after a mawkish interlude with Bloom's muse, the calendar-art nymph on his bedroom wall. Virtually restored and saved from the depths of himself, Bloom has a final relatively mild hallucination, participating in Boylan's seduction of Molly as an exaggerated version of that comic byword, the complacent husband. The whole experience, though it dominates the chapter, has taken relatively little time, but it has steeled Bloom for what is to come: the encounter with Stephen and his return to Molly's bed. Having capitulated to impulses that crippled him, he is free to resume a role that is both dominant in him and appropriate.

As Bloom emerges from his last hallucination, Lynch makes the equation that signals a transfer of our attention to Stephen, pointing to the mirror in which both are joined in the likeness of Shakespeare under the antlered hatrack (567).[14] Stephen, who begins by raving incoherently, spewing out the garbled contents of the day's thoughts, finally breaks into his drunken dance and begins hallucinating aloud. Having previously taken Stephen's money in safe keeping (seconding in this the advice of old Deasy, his precursor, and inverting the behavior of the pawnbroker Dodd, his dark reflection), a masterful Bloom pays the damages after the attack on the lampshade and runs out into the street. He arrives too late to prevent the fight, but still manages to fend off the police while Stephen lies in a drunken stupor. It is at this point that the symbolic link between the two men is confirmed by Bloom's vision of Rudy as an eleven-year-old Pre-Raphaelite dream child with a ''mauve'' face, a ghastly-sweet emanation hovering over the prostrate poet. The moment is worthy of the Dublin Christmas Pantomime, but the reader may be moved as well as amused and shocked.[15]

Concerned and eager to help, anxious to make contact with the youth he has identified with his son, Bloom escorts the sodden bard to the nearby cabman's shelter for undrinkable coffee and an inedible bun. Thanks to the presence of a returning sailor who spins improbable traveler's tales, conversation is difficult if not impossible. Still, for the first time this day, Bloom is in command of the fate of another whom he respects, and, though tired, he is more than usually alert and talkative. Stephen, by contrast, distracted and bored, speaks rarely and at cross purposes with Bloom. Seizing on the fact that his protégé claims to have eaten nothing for over a day (656), Bloom decides to offer him a bed for the night and brave Molly's wrath. As they walk home together, Stephen warms to a discussion of music and begins singing, inspiring the practical-minded Bloom to outline the advantages of a musical career. During the song, the older man completes the transition to fatherhood by echoing in milder and muddier terms Simon Dedalus' opinion of Mulligan's influence:

> . . . he purposed (Bloom did), without anyway prying into his private affairs on the *fools step in where angels* principle advising him to sever his connections with a certain budding practitioner, who, he noticed, was prone to disparage, and even, . . . with some hilarious pretext, . . . deprecate him. . . . (664–65)

In response to this, a horse mires and Stephen maunders about "usurpers."

At 7 Eccles Street ("Ithaca"), Bloom shows Stephen into the kitchen, makes two cups of cocoa, lacing Stephen's generously with Molly's breakfast cream, a further sign of new-won independence. Their conversation turns on their common backgrounds, their differences, and the similarities that underlie them (see the delightful equation of the Jewish and Irish traditions [688].) It is only after Stephen has sung his anti-Semitic ballad that the "secret infidel" Bloom offers him a bed and accepts his refusal. After Stephen's departure through the gate, unlocked by an "aruginated male key," Bloom must face the facts he has been avoiding. This he does in the fashion of a returned wanderer, taking inventory first of his worldly situation, inspecting (?) documents that relate his past, observing the evidence of another's usurpation, and deciding what is to be done about it (nothing). Brushing the remains of Boylan's picnic from his bed, he kisses Molly's rump, gives her a slightly modified account of his day, and lies down head to her feet to sleep, a wary, much-traveled Sinbad. He has asked her to "get his breakfast in bed with a couple of eggs" (738) and mentioned a possible future association with Stephen. Joyce's "Gea-

Tellus,'' the great mother to whose womb Bloom returns, then begins the musings out of which, for all his failings, the returned traveler emerges her man, the one to whom she has once said, "Yes."

Molly, the Necessary Countersign

The male world of Stephen and Bloom is characteristically incomplete. ("What is a home without Plumtree's Potted Meat" reads the insistent ad.) Enclosed all day by the four walls of her house and room, served by Bloom and an inefficient servant, acted upon more than acting, a presence, an emanation but a mastering force as well, Molly complements our sense of the two men, helps to unite them. Throughout his day, Stephen behaves as though everything is an aspect of his self, and his soul is indeed the Aristotelian "form of forms." Bloom, on the other hand, sees himself in relation to the world, while Molly, completing the trinity, perceives the world as relating to her. In her devastatingly frank monologue, she reveals herself as *das ewig Weibliche,* but as such she is a product of the male imagination as well as a person in her own right. Because of the way she is presented throughout the book and in terms of the larger symbolic structure of *Ulysses,* we are right to see her as the great whore even though she rejects the role and seems in fact to have indulged in nothing more than harmless flirtations during Bloom's long sexual absence.

Curiously, it is Molly, fresh from Boylan's embraces, who testifies to Bloom's sexual prowess and rehabilitates him in our eyes, but paradoxically, it is the thought of a possible liaison with the "young professor" that inspires memories of the younger Leopold trying to look like Byron, and that *may* even draw the couple together again. Before the extended exposure in "Penelope," we see Molly only briefly as Calypso, but her presence is felt everywhere Bloom goes. We get to know her as Bloom knows her and as others think they know her. For Bloom she is all, the omphalos about which he turns anxiously, the womb to which he returns, and the genetrix of his possible progeny. Stephen, on the other hand, yearns for her as the Oedipal mate who will help fill the void left by his mother's death, complete his manhood, and perhaps mend his breeches before turning him out into the world.

Curiously, it is this sort of relationship he rejects in "Ithaca," as Molly realizes through her monologue in "Penelope."

> I wonder why he wouldnt stay the night . . . he could easy have slept in there on the sofa in the other room I suppose he was as shy as a boy he being so young hardly 20 of me in the next room hed have heard me on the chamber arrah what harm . . . Id have to introduce myself not knowing me from Adam very funny wouldnt it Im his wife . . . itd be great fun supposing he stayed with us why not theres the room upstairs . . . Id love to have a long talk with an intelligent well-educated person Id have to get a nice pair of red slippers like those Turks with the fez used to sell or yellow and a nice semi-transparent morning gown that I badly want or a peachblossom dressing jacket like the one long ago in Walpoles only 8/6 or 18/6 Ill just give him one more chance . . . (778–80)

A circle would seem to have been closed by the last sentence, which reverts from Stephen to Bloom after Molly has united Stephen's dream of the East and Bloom's vision of her in Eastern dress. The offer of melons ("melon he had he held to my face . . . Come. Red carpet spread" [47].) has been refused "promptly, inexplicably, with amicability" (695) by Stephen but accepted by Bloom in Stephen's place, fulfilling both men, settling nothing, preparing the way for the sun to rise in the East. So much progress has been made.

Though apparently the least inhibited of them all, despite her appetites and bold talk Molly has a rigid moral system. Joyce is playing here with the relationship of innocence to guilt, flesh to spirit, and sterility to fertility in the person of Calpe's daughter Marion, who may be as natural but is certainly not as free as her namesake saluted by Mercurial Malachi at breakfast:

> —*For old Mary Ann*
> *She doesn't care a damn,*
> *But, hising up her petticoats* . . . (13)

It is worth noting that she spends more time justifying her fall in terms of Bloom's failures than she does reminiscing about her sexual adventures, that Boylan and Bloom are paired in her mind as sexual objects, that she is shocked by her own coarse language and seems to prefer euphemisms, and that she prefers Bloom in the end and makes a remarkably good case for her preference. Subject though she is to lunar influences (see the menstruation which takes her in the middle of her monologue), she represents the stable goal of male striving as well as the impulse that generates it. With logic, Joyce's schema identifies her with earth or substance and sees the web of words she spins (or the web of her attraction) as motion, for Stephen sees "movement" through Aristotle's definition as the "actuality of the possible as possible" (25), and Molly is the image of the word actualized as flesh.

In *Finnegans Wake* the metaphor is expanded. Anna Livia Plurabelle, the primal Mother, is at once the destroyer, the prolonger, and the protector of her all-Father husband Humphrey Chimpden Earwicker, supporter of the material universe. As daughter, Issy-Isolde, she tempts and betrays her father-husband Mark of Cornwall. As wife, she bears him 111 children. As the old hag, Kate the slop, she keens over him, buries him, and distributes his substance to his children. As defender and muse, she dictates the book or letter of life to her writer son, Shem the pen, a later version of the starveling Stephen, just as the boisterous Shaun the post, who delivers the letter, is a later version of Buck Mulligan (among others).

III

Two Characters and a City-Scape

Stephen/Bloom: Opposite Equivalents

If, under Joyce's microscope, Bloom personifies everyman as outsider, his position is not unmotivated. Incapable of servicing Molly, and essentially estranged from his daughter as love object, too self-deprecating and insufficiently imaginative to "succeed" but too abstemious and industrious to fail totally, too obviously alien and cosmopolitan to be accepted by the Irish provincials and too Irish not to be concerned, he is doomed to a perpetual search for the center, which for him means balance. Seen from another angle, in a society peopled by eccentrics, the outrageously moderate Bloom must seem peculiar. Unlike Stephen, the rebel who consciously courts rejection, Bloom must tread warily in the face of rejection. He tempts no gods, risks no thunderous retribution, accepts his lot, and returns good for evil. Though the memory of his father's suicide darkens his day and he contacts madness through Mr. Breen, he risks neither. His main concern is to hang on to the social norm, to confirm his position as father, husband, citizen, in a world that repulses his advances on all fronts. He is out of phase with his society and antiheroic in his adjustment, but he is without pride or cynicism or pretense. Gross pragmatism, while occasionally a source of wisdom, more often leads him clownishly to overvalue trifles that Stephen just as absurdly ignores. His treatment of the cake of soap, the flower, the card, his preoccupation with numbers, food, manners, and facts tend to make Bloom himself an object among objects and prepare us for his eventual reduction to a catalogue of particulars in "Ithaca."

We watch through the daylight hours Bloom's growing preoccupation with a little knot of closely-related and virtually universal concerns, which, during the evening hours, he faces on an instinctual level. But if on this day the meaning of the key to his house is made manifest to him, his worries make few visible ripples on the calm surface. Faced with Molly's infidelity and possible desertion, Milly's coming of age, and his failure to produce a son, haunted by the memory of his father and his own lack of a tradition in tradition-bound Ireland, he finds relief in exceptional social and mental activity. Individually, given their history and Bloom's disposition, none of these concerns is particularly grave. Coalescing under the heading "function," they demand some sort of resolution, for they constitute the everyman's reason for being. But given his peculiar relationship to Molly and the world, Bloom can do nothing about them. In the end, action takes the form of passive resignation or adjustment, the acceptance of the inevitable as inevitable. Bloom has come as close as he can to self-discovery and to the restoration of his manhood. In the process he has incriminated and cleansed each of us of a variety of lusts and anguishes.

Though we find ourselves agreeing with Bloom's judgments, identifying with his foibles, understanding his errors, siding with him against adversaries, and preferring him over his peers, we are never allowed to forget his comic identity, to lose perspective or distance. His frustrations, conflicts, aspirations, inadequacies, fears, and joys are always comic on a relative scale, just as his actions are often rendered funny by the reactions of others to them. When, among the outhouse fumes, he pictures himself a writer of pulp fiction and then wipes himself with his model's story; when, busily researching the Keyes advertisement, he mixes with the learned in the library; when, intent on seeing a woman's silk-stockinged calf, he is frustrated by a passing tram; when, against the citizen's monumental chauvinism and terrible envy, he preaches fair play and Christian love to the gentiles in Barney Kiernan's pub; when, in short, he pursues an infinitude of unworthy ends and brushes off innumerable slights and injuries, he plays the endearing fool in our eyes.

Perhaps the secret of Bloom's success lies in the fact that many of the shocks he deals to our sensibility are shocks of recognition light enough for us to endure and that the blows he receives bruise but do not break his spirit. Our introduction to the sensual man, coming as it does after our initiation into Stephen's perturbed and rarefied intellect is more like a warm bath than a cold shower. It may take a while for us to recognize ourselves in the kidney-eater who sees the cat's "lithe black form," and "the gloss of her sleek hide" and then pointedly notes "the white button under the butt of her tail." But after the metaphor-ridden thoughtstream of Stephen, Bloom's commonsense cat's-eye view of himself as a giant is endearing: "Wonder what I look like to her. Height of a tower? No, she can jump me" (55). Muffing an opportunity to assert his superiority, he has reduced himself to human size and proclaimed his vulnerability. Never straining for the right word, the precise thought, Bloom coasts along seeing only what is there and telling himself, never others, what he sees (as opposed to what he thinks). By contrast, Joyce has made Stephen uncharitable and unapproachable, though admirable—the consummate ironist.

Unlike the traditional butt of comic or farcical laughter, Bloom has been turned into a surrogate perceiver and reactor for the unwary reader. In this he is very different too from the traditional first person narrator or even the modern unreliable narrator, both of whom set out to win our applause. To the extent that he comes to us through his stream of consciousness, he comes as one unaware of our presence and unprepared to make a play for sympathy. (It is appropriate that when Bloom makes a public bid for sympathy in "Cyclops," "Oxen of the Sun," or "Eumaeus," his companions respond negatively.) Perhaps Joyce has succeeded in making him seem a "good" man, for the expression in unguarded moments of his true and valid motives combined with his generous spirit, his freedom from cant, and his sharply focussed humorous view of life endear him to us as the habits of a canting Conmee and a crass Kernan in "Wandering Rocks" do not. Repeatedly, we share his unexpressed pain and distress and experience without sentimentality what relief is possible for him. We may even feel for him, what he cannot feel for himself, a painful embarrassment over his pleasures and tastes or a vague sadness over his failure to see his weakness vis-à-vis Stephen or to appreciate his strength in relation to Molly. Beyond all of this is our sense that Bloom is bigger than life, that he has been deliberately overdrawn as a monster of normality. The result is comedy, yes, but a comedy generously sprinkled with pathos which, like so much that is modern, turns back on the reader almost as much as it does on the weak, blind, foolish, or stunted protagonist.

The fact that we know more about Bloom as a sentient human being than we do about any other literary hero does not set him apart. Quite the contrary, it underlines his role as the unexceptional man, *l'homme moyen sensuel* in Montaigne's famous phrase, a figure who experiences but does not capitulate to exceptional desires, who takes life as it comes, who expresses to himself what he prudently leaves unsaid, and who represses what he fears to admit or face, a man who is neither brave nor cowardly. But every man is in some way separate from the crowd and Bloom is doubly distinguished, being not only a potential cuckold but a Jew in Dublin. A norm for the world—the city man—he is nevertheless a fringe figure and an outsider in his own city if not in his own eyes. Joyce makes good use of this condition, which gives Bloom enough distance from his fellows to make him a perfect commentator on their foibles but leaves him Irish enough and mature enough to show understanding and sympathy. Like Stephen's Shakespeare, he is more than just another husband in what the unmarried John Eglinton calls a "French triangle," just as he is more than that cliché of Jewish humor, the Jew who takes it from all comers—a cultural Pierrot. For one thing he is an accomplice in his fate as well as a victim, for another he has not given up hope or resorted to acts of comic desperation. He is also one who suffers for his indecision, a trait he shares with Stephen, but, unlike Stephen and like the majority of men, he is not sufficiently aware of himself to understand the nature of the decisions he could make or to question the psychological motivation for his errors.

Using Kierkegaard's categories, Arnold Goldman[1] has perceptively defined Stephen in terms of his attitude as the "ironic" man and Bloom as the "comic" man. An example might help clarify this distinction. Bloom with humorous pathos accepts the death of a casual friend, saying "Poor Dignam," and with distanced anguish says "Poor Papa" about his father, old and alone, deserted in the West of Ireland and sad enough to take a poisonous overdose of medicine. Stephen, haunted too by his personal ghost, is clearly incapable of saying with genuine or distanced sympathy "poor mother," and instead is forced to avenge her death on his own spirit while defending himself against the charge of matricide like a Fury-ridden Orestes. The one man in his weakness recognizes the world in which he has no power, the other in his strength sees the world as within himself, and himself as responsible. Neither position is completely adequate, but Stephen's is intolerable if not tragic while Bloom's is simply undistinguished. Accordingly, still certain of his potential but emasculated by the ghost of his own inadequacy and feeling cheated of his spiritual patrimony, Stephen wanders about "reading the book of himself." Despair and guilt have left him almost as unsure of his artistic vocation as he once was of his priestly one. However, if Bloom's assurance is the product of ignorance and limited capacities, Stephen's confusion is the confusion of brilliance and too much knowledge. Discontented with and frustrated by the ideals toward which his art and learning point, but unable to accept the world, which could save him, he has turned to the Devil and become Mulligan's man. During his day he walks painfully in the Buck's cast-off boots, testing the alternatives which his talents leave open to him: teaching, journalism, scholarship, singing, living by his wits. Since he sees only desolation in his future and unpaid debts in his past, he is incapable of accepting or rejecting these temptations. It is his best qualities, his honesty and pride, that make him a bitter brooder and an ascetic rather than a carefree hedonist like Mulligan or an amoral sponge like Lynch. As a result, he is what the Buck calls an "impossible person" (9) whose cynicism and irony are a negative faith which alone saves him from maudlin despair. The grotesque mock-heroic climax of "Circe" seems inevitable. The appropriate ironic response to a reasoned failure to take a stand is mindless action. He must be reduced and freed of his rational self so that he can make the gestures of rejection that will symbolically recapitulate the conclusion of the *Portrait*, obliterate what followed that false start, and restore him to youth and sanity. It matters and it does not matter that these gestures are no more than drunken maunderings, a pantomime of action, that he himself is unconsciously wearing at that moment the mask not of the artist-hero but of the pathetic clown, and that he neither breaks the light of the world nor holds his own in an argument against force. (Christ after all faced a similar failure and Hamlet achieved his goal only by inadvertence.) The climax of "Circe" approximates a tragic denouement, a moment of truth, a purging that should be followed at least in the mind of the reader by a theophany or elevation, suggested both by Bloom's vision of Rudy and by their shaky rapport in "Eumaeus" and "Ithaca," and confirmed in "Penelope." But Joyce's tragedy is in a minor key, jocular tragedy not to be taken *too* lightly, and what Stephen needs is not the father Mulligan says he seeks or the motherly woman he misses, but self assurance, a sense of humor, and objectivity, qualities possessed by Bloom in good measure.

Bloom and Stephen, by nature and/or nurture exiles and opposites, are emotional father and son, but each needs the other in himself far more than in the flesh. It is with the younger Bloom, revitalized by her meditations on Stephen, that Molly may resume her relations. It is with his own mature self engaged by the world that Stephen may hopefully identify. Through concern for himself (a self he has habitually neglected), Bloom has obliged Molly to reconsider her rejection of him. After his experiment with sound in "Proteus," Stephen opens his eyes to find the world "there all the time without" him but then immediately translates the temporal into the eternal, adding "and ever shall be, world without end" (37). What Stephen needs is an awareness of the here and now. On the pragmatic level, though exile is a permanent and necessary condition for Stephen as artist and Bloom as Jew in Ireland, each can modify his adjustment. Bloom can live within the society into which he was born; accommodating himself to a split world-view and facing up to past failures, he may even resume an ambiguous marital arrangement in a position of strength. Stephen can either decide to exist in a Dublin all of whose many facets are personally repugnant and obnoxious to his still distant goals as artist or he can reject his guilt and allegiances along with offers of an easier life and, with his eyes open this time, make an unromantic second flight. Both must adjust in terms of Ireland (and Dublin), which becomes a middle term, a comitragic country that produces heroes and betrayers in equal numbers and a superabundance of dreamers and clowns.

A Human Landscape

Among Joyce's most astonishing feats is his vital and engaging portrait of Dublin as a modern commercial and cultural capital, ironically analogous to all cities in all ages. Dublin is a backdrop for action, a projection of Joyce's major protagonists, and a persona, which, like Stephen and Bloom, experiences a full day and night of life and exposes many facets of its personality. Though Stephen and Bloom are respectively a temperamental and a social outcast, and though they function within opposite sectors of the community, neither man occupies an extreme position in relation to a society that welcomes the one and barely tolerates the other. We see them reacting to and experiencing the essential life of a community which shades off from their positions towards fringes which are barely glimpsed. Still, between them, they survey and expose the world of commerce, journalism, education, music, and literature. With them we visit a school, the library, a newspaper office, the cemetery, a hospital, a whore house; we walk the streets and beaches, number the shops, inspect the monuments, watch (and once ride) the trams, sample food and drink, and engage in conversations relevant to the concerns of the day. They take us from birth to death, from the church to the pub, from the bachelor's quarters to the home, from the pleasures and preoccupations of students and young dilettantes to those of the mature and settled if slightly seedy citizens. Joyce's pragmatic vision of Dublin is designed to put everything in its proper place. He is careful not to locate the center of the city, its heart, but he is also careful to put more emphasis on Bloom's world, on the world of normal social intercourse and popular culture, epitomized on the positive side by Simon Dedalus and on the negative by the narrator of "Cyclops."

Stephen's father stands out as one of Joyce's great creations from life, a remarkably complete man given to us through his words and actions in four contexts and through the disparate responses of the major protagonists. A wastrel but not a scamp or a cheat, a wit but not devoid of sympathy, a gifted singer and popular figure too lazy and dissolute to capitalize on his gifts, a potential womanizer who is no *roué,* a man at once selfish and self-pitying but one also capable of the gracious manner and full of the sap of life, a poor father who meditates bitterly on the company his son keeps but lets his family go hungry while he escapes through talk and drink, a bad husband who sentimentally mourns the wife he worked to death, Simon is, more than any other character, an embodiment of the graces and vices of Dublin. It is appropriate that, though he and Bloom have little real common ground, Simon occupies a central position in Bloom's world and that through him Stephen's and Bloom's social universes are momentarily joined. The relationship is confirmed along with Simon's character by Molly, whose epigrammatic characterizations are extraordinarily apt:

> . . . such a criticiser with his glasses up with his tall hat on him at the cricket match and a great big hole in his sock one thing laughing at the other and his son that got all those prizes for whatever . . . imagine [Poldy] climbing over the railings if anybody saw him that knew us wonder he didnt tear a big hole in his grand funeral trousers. . . . (768)

If we place Simon and his mildly genteel and gently improvident cronies in the center of Joyce's Dublin, the rest of the portrait follows logically but not mechanically. With the cool eye of an insider and the terse expression of a born raconteur, the thirsty dun of "Cyclops" gives us a whole range of lower middle class life and what is perhaps an unfair sampling of the revolutionary mentality. Other intersecting worlds are represented by other methods. Father Conmee, the former rector of Clongowes Wood school, one of Stephen's earlier fathers, and one of Joyce's sharpest satirical tools, supplements the glimpses of Dublin's spiritual life we get through Bloom in "Lestrygonians" and Gerty MacDowell in "Nausikaa." Gerty, who gives us the world of Irish single girls which she shares with Milly Bloom and the sirens in the Ormond bar, is in her turn supplemented by Molly in her reminiscences. Small boys are represented by Master Patrick Aloysius Dignam, a pale reflection of Stephen's Catholic childhood, who supplements the scene at Deasy's school and Stephen's own recollections.

Joyce's researches into the practical details of Dublin life, his fidelity to the data in Thom's Dublin Directory, have become proverbial, so much so that critics have made capital of his occasional lapses.[2] In searching to convey the distinctive nature of the city enshrined in his memory, he outdid himself and earlier realists. It is almost a tribute to his success that a disturbed Dubliner once said to me, "but you know he hasn't shown the real Dublin." It is obvious that he hasn't shown the Dublin any one man would accept as his city, anymore than he has in Bloom portrayed a man with whom we can completely identify. But he has created a city that grows on us and exceeds itself. Any Dubliner can point to places, types, or customs slighted, but no one can deny the vitality of this canvas that shades off from the center toward the excesses of poverty and wealth, madness and death, gives us the contrasting public and private worlds, and lets the day fade into the night. But the Dublin that we have is a Dublin that we make, assembling the pieces in whatever order suits us, in a manner that echoes Joyce's method in "Wandering Rocks," where the juxtaposed vignettes are cemented by the interjection of parallel events.

As a town, Dublin takes life as much from its role in the day of Stephen, Bloom, and Molly as from thousands of trivial but vivid details that constitute its substance, but it is not only a projection of their experience of it, it is also a projection of their experience of themselves. Each character, no matter how vivid he is in his own right, exists in terms of Bloom and Stephen, and some characters, while fulfilling minor roles in the book, exist most emphatically as aspects of what these two wanderers are and projections of what they might be. The technique is not a new one. We find variations on it in Tolstoi, who sets up elaborate foils complete with antithetical contexts; in Balzac, who permits the "minor" characters of *Père Goriot* to pump life into his hero Rastignac; in Flaubert's *Sentimental Education,* where the life Frédéric Moreau only samples is lived in detail by a gallery of acquaintances almost as large as the cast of *Ulysses;* and in chapter 5 of the *Portrait,* where each of Stephen's friends represents both an aspect of the Ireland Stephen will leave and an indication of a direction he might otherwise follow.

Thanks partly to the dramatic method which allows Joyce to present characters without explicit commentary, we have in *Ulysses* an astonishing range of vivid individuals among the minor figures. These latter shade off almost imperceptibly from the vigorously presented Mulligan, to the shadowy loners, lunatics, and ghosts who seem to define the limits of the knowable world but who embody during the daylight hours the norms of the night and the repressed impulses of normal people. At one extreme we have our anti-Stephens or our anti-Blooms; at the other we have creatures turning into symbols, contributing to theme or merging with the landscape: Mrs. M'Guinness the plump pawnbroker and her Italianate namesake Denis J. Maginni, bald-deaf Pat the waiter, an old milk woman, a pugnosed tram driver, an affectionate policeman, lackeys, and even animals. Each of these lesser figures is distinguished by a single act or attribute or epiphanized by Joyce's quick pen as in the following two portraits from "Hades":

> Mourners came out through the gates: woman and a girl. Leanjawed harpy, hard woman at a bargain, her bonnet awry. Girl's face stained with dirt and tears, holding the woman's arm looking up at her for a sign to cry. Fish's face, bloodless and livid.
>
> Coffin now . . . Horse looking round at it with his plume skeowways. Dull eye: collar tight on his neck, pressing on a bloodvessel or something. (101)[3]

Little more is seen of some minor characters who serve as foils for Stephen and Bloom. Still we have a sense of the individuality of Reuben J. Dodd (an embodiment of the avaricious Jew and the bad father, an object of hatred),[4] Denis Breen (a projection of madness, a failed man, and an object of ridicule), or Mr. Purefoy (the prim Protestant progenitor and proper lower middle class Dubliner, who knows how to keep his wife faithful). Breen, whose name contains the same number of vowels and consonants as Bloom's, is emphatically associated with him as a "Half and half . . . that's neither fish nor flesh" in "Cyclops" (321). Breen spends his day wandering the streets of Dublin in a vain attempt to redress a grievance against the sender of an anonymous postcard containing nothing but the letters "U.P." Like Dodd and Purefoy, he never occupies the foreground and like them he is identifiable as a Pantaloon, the *Commedia dell' Arte* Merchant of Venice: "And begob what was it only that bloody old pantaloon Denis Breen in his bath slippers with two bloody big books tucked under his oxter ..." (298). Joyce is of course playing with and against a stereotype which figures also in Stephen's discussion of Shakespeare and is inevitably identified with Bloom as cuckold, Jew, and dupe. The symbolic and analogical identities do not, however, rob Breen of verisimilitude. This pathetic little lunatic is seen from at least four angles. As husband, rival, citizen, and fixated madman, he takes life from his surroundings and from what we see of his life through the keyhole: "Cruelty to animals so it is," the narrator of "Cyclops" reflects in response to Bloom's plea for sympathy for Josie Breen,

> to let that bloody povertystricken Breen out on grass with his beard out tripping him, bringing down the rain. And she with her nose cockahoop after she married him because a cousin of his old fellow's was pew opener to the pope. Picture of him on the wall with his smashall sweeney's moustaches. (321)

Stephen, who feels more threatened by madness than Bloom, finds his mad surrogate in the "constant reader" Cashell Boyle O'Connor Fitzmaurice Tisdall Farrell, the dwarfish scion of an exhausted line, who "parafes his polysyllables" in "Scylla." Following as it does the Shakespeare discussion, during which Stephen forces himself into Hamlet's boots, Farrell's appearance is ominous: "Item: was Hamlet mad?" Stephen asks himself (215). It is important that during "Lestrygonians," where Josie compares him to Breen, Bloom sees Farrell walking "outside the lampposts" wearing a "tiny hat" that "gripped his head" like a "skullpiece" (159).

By dint of juxtapositions and thematic or verbal echoes, Joyce manages to link such disparate integers as the younger Dodd (the suicidal son rejected by Simon in Bloom's presence), the "blind stripling" (a cane-carrying "absentminded beggar," who leaves his tuning fork at the Ormond and accidentally bumps into an enraged Farrell), and Farrell himself. The network of relationships need not stop there. Any reader can find legitimate ways of linking characters contributing to the various themes of the book, which in turn are generally linked to the major protagonists' main preoccupations. We have among other things groups of ghosts, of suicides or drownings, of moneylenders, of clowns and fools, of spoiled priests, and of inadequate servants; and none of these groups needs to be validated by the fascinating but tenuous analogical systems to which they all inevitably contribute. Other minor characters represent not alternate trades or traits but alternate routes for Bloom or Stephen: the panhandler, Corley (one of the "Two Gallants" in *Dubliners*), who importunes Stephen in "Eumaeus," the Frenchified exile, Patrice Egan, whose character is highlighted in "Proteus," and the gentle, effeminate esthete and toady, Mr. Best, who featly foots it through the library. Such relationships, and there are many more, help identify the protagonists in terms of Dublin and the shifting scene. They also emphasize those qualities or preoccupations of which they are extreme examples, setting Stephen and Bloom (and Molly, who must be related to other women) in a more normal light. For all their individuality and despite the facts that make them exiles in the community, Stephen, Bloom, and Molly are very Irish in quirky Dublin, where every third individual is an eccentric though only the exceptional few make capital of their quirks.

Blazes/Buck: Solar Shadows

Chief among these exceptions are Mulligan and Boylan, "sunny" Buck and solar Blazes, a looking-glass couple of sufficient stature to function as opposite equivalents and rivals of the somber and lunar Stephen and Bloom. We may suspect that Boylan is Mulligan reduced to the crudest terms, the flashy vulgarian as opposed to the vulgar dandy, for Mulligan, like Wilde, is something of a "pretender" or poseur. Like Stephen, he seems to wear a mask which we can pierce only occasionally, as when he shows anxiety over Stephen's grievance in "Telemachus": "A light wind passed his brow, fanning softly his fair uncombed hair and stirring silver points of anxiety in his eyes" (8). At such moments we understand Stephen's attachment to him or to the hidden frailty revealed in this case through a trick of light. There is also strength and generosity, vigour and wit. Mulligan has saved a man from drowning. He will give willingly, though ostentatiously, of his substance and as willingly accept. He can praise as well as scorn. These are all qualities admired and resented by Stephen, whose courage and generosity are muted by terror and insecurity and whose pride forces him to accept the gift while rejecting the giver.

Buck takes his nickname from an eighteenth century Dublin rake, but the name also suggests the goat of lechery and whimsy, a joyous but unstable and treacherous figure whose very gestures he imitates in "Telemachus": "He capered before them . . . fluttering his winglike hands, leaping nimbly" (19). Joyce spares no pains to make him appealing (in complete contrast to the gloomy and self-obsessed Stephen), gratuitously but delightfully witty and obscene, cultivated but not pedantic, full of himself but insouciant in his "primrose waistcoat." When he enters even the most dismal room, we experience the lift given when sunlight pierces the clouds. He is indeed "tripping and sunny" with his "yellow dressinggown," his goldpointed white teeth (Stephen's are rotten), his airy manner, and his enviable vocabulary of amusing gestures. Mulligan practices effortlessly, if frivolously, the art which Stephen, going J. K. Huysmans and the Symbolists one better, preaches in "Circe": "So that gesture, not music, not odours, would be a universal language, the gift of tongues rendering visible not the lay sense but the first entelechy, the structural rhythm" (432). Buck also practices with gracious and disconcerting facility the arts of poetry and rhetoric, while enjoying financial independence and the prospect of a secure future as a doctor. Despite himself, Stephen sees in him an enviable model. Throughout the day, we see him desperately but mistakenly trying to imitate the Buck's contagious charm, to assume his mask as earlier he has assumed others: "Proudly walking," he recalls in "Proteus." "Whom were you trying to walk like? Forget: a dispossessed" (41). As a performer Stephen predictably fails. His is the "darkness shining in brightness" (48) that brightness fails to comprehend. His wit is ironic, biting, pointed, and never gratuitous—the scholastic's "lancet" (7). He seems automatically, though not without bitterness, to assume the role of victim which he shares with Bloom, just as Mulligan shares with Boylan the role of sunny conqueror. Formerly, he has welcomed Cranly as a secular confessor; now he accepts his subservience to Buck as an emblem of shame and a symbol of failure. It is characteristic that Mulligan is unaware of this and insensitive to his friend's feelings, but so polished is his mask of mindless and carefree folly, that he has earned the fool's privileges and his license goes unpunished.

Buck appears to have seduced the very muse that sent Stephen winging to Paris. During his day Stephen manages to produce only a miserable quatrain written on a scrap of paper torn from Deasy's hoof and mouth letter:

> *On swift sail flaming*
> *From storm and south*
> *He comes, pale vampire,*
> *Mouth to my mouth.* (132)

(It is characteristic of Joyce's irony that he identifies the paper used by Stephen with the prize story used by the aspiring pulp fiction writer, Bloom, in his privy.) Buck, on the other hand, turns out clever, off-color spoofs effortlessly and broadcasts them to the amused mob. He is what Dublin would call an "artist," meaning the accomplished jokester.[5] There is however another side to his character: his literary and perhaps personal decadence. From the start he is identified with the art and person of Oscar Wilde[6] as opposed to the lushly erotic and masochistic Swinburne, whom he quotes but whom Joyce pairs with Stephen. Mulligan, the faddist and exhibitionist, a man who, like Wilde, would be apt to make his life his art, is the worst possible exemplar and the most dangerous rival for one who feels he must elaborate out of himself painfully, in the manner of Shem the pen,[7] and who has dedicated himself to "silence, exile, and cunning."[8] The full extent of the danger is illustrated by the brief scene in "Wandering Rocks" where the erstwhile friend and supporter tells Haines of Stephen's absurd plan to "write something in ten years" (249). Friendship with Mulligan, were there any stability in it, might lead to acceptance in Ireland, but it constitutes in fact an inhibition to freedom. Buck becomes in the course of this book the prime symbol of the forces trying to shape Stephen into what he cannot be, forces toward which Stephen feels dangerously drawn: "Staunch friend, a brother soul: Wilde's love that dare not speak its name. He now will leave me. And the blame? As I am. As I am. All or not at all" (49). The reference to "Wilde's love," or homosexuality, points up a final aspect of the relationship, which Stephen would reject as he has formerly rejected Cranly, an aspect that colors both the Shakespeare argument and Stephen's contact with Bloom.

Unlike Stephen, who seems to choose his torments, Bloom is the passive victim of his weaknesses. Unlike Mulligan, who is much less "bad" than his words suggest, Boylan is the physical usurper, the vulgar seducer whose virility Bloom envies and fears. It is comically appropriate that, after he has played the seducer in a minor key to Gerty, Bloom finds himself identifying masochistically with the gaudily dressed conquerer: "Us too: the tie he wore, his lovely socks and turnedup trousers. He wore a pair of gaiters the night that first we met. His lovely shirt was shining beneath his what? of jet" (369). As a reflection on Bloom's own weakness, the lover's actions are in a sense controlled by the husband's inaction. He is the classic fancyman, the gay seducer of the wives of negligent husbands, the hero of countless bedroom farces, the idol of the lesser pub characters and the shopgirls. But he is more: a caricature of the type, cruder, bolder, dumber, a Dublin "billsticker."

An operator, a speculator who trades on Dublin's foibles, who even plays at being an impresario, Boylan is still a brightly colored, jaunty, jingling Harlequin. Joyce presents him obliquely, through the eyes and reactions of characters who hardly know him, as a self-centered fellow, a loner who passes frequently but seldom stops to chat. He speaks in fact a bare handful of words and remains a figment of the public imagination. Bloom draws him out of the pornographic books he reads and confuses him with a variety of subliterary types. Even Molly can depict only the sexual animal, speaking with mixed admiration and distaste of his performance and his lapses into grossness and rage.

But there is no need to complete the stereotype which stands in opposition to the most developed character in literature and paradoxically draws life from the ultrasophisticated Mulligan, Bloom's rival for the affections of Stephen. The two figures from opposite cultural milieux help, like Stephen and Bloom, to describe the centers of which they are extreme examples. Thus the bounder who knows how to use the commercial, the sporting, and the musical centers which accept him in full awareness of the liberties he takes, is as much a measure of these aspects of Dublin as Mulligan is of the intellectual, professional, and artistic worlds whose measurements he takes. Joyce has neatly circumscribed his city with his four compass points projected against a subtly realized physical and spiritual map.

IV

Adjuncts to Meaning

Joyce's "Odyssey"

We cannot ignore the fact that Joyce modeled *Ulysses* after *The Odyssey*. He made this clear when he named his book and inescapable when he gave Herbert Gorman his schema and encouraged Stuart Gilbert to explore the analogy in detail. But like Vergil before him, he has taken enormous liberties with his model, while, unlike Vergil, he has neither created a second Ulysses nor set Homer's hero up as the embodiment of unalloyed virtue. Though we may pass over many of the details of the schema, which points up Joyce's preoccupation with universals (the human organism, the components of life, the hours and phases of a day, the arts of man, etc.), we must accept and deal with the analogical implications latent in the homeric title, episodes, and characters, for to a degree they dictated the form of the book, and even now they clarify the nature of the heroes' quests and identities. Joyce chose Homer's hero as his model for Bloom because Ulysses was to his mind the most complete character in literature, a figure seen from many points of view, engaged in many activities in terms of his many functions. Like Ulysses, Bloom is, according to Joyce, "a complete man" as well as a "good man," though not necessarily ideal.[1] The word "good," as suggestive as it is vague, doubtless applies also to the world Joyce surveys, if we are to take Molly Bloom's final "yes" in its fullest sense.

Ulysses' three subdivisions, the "Telemachia," the "Odyssey," and the "Nostos" (i.e., the return), correspond to the three main

61

sections of *The Odyssey*. Joyce's first three chapters approximate
Homer's account of how Telemachus, awakened to manhood by
Athena, goes out into the world to test his powers and discover
what can be learned about his father's whereabouts. The twelve
chapters of the central section roughly parallel Homer's account of
Ulysses' departure from Calypso, the nymph who has kept him
prisoner of love, and his visit with the Phaeacians to whom he tells
the tale of his travels and misfortunes before they transport him
back to Ithaca. In the "Nostos," Joyce's Ulysses reveals himself to
his "son." Together they slaughter the suitors so that the hero
may regain his kingdom, rejoin his faithful and long-suffering
Penelope, and set out on his final quest.

At once delightfully literal in his reading and boldly free with his
model, Joyce took joy in establishing ironic and interpretative
analogies for even the least of Homer's details:

> I am now writing the *Lestrygonians* episode, which corre-
> sponds to the adventure of Ulysses with the cannibals. My
> hero is going to lunch. But there is a seduction motive in
> the Odyssey, the cannibal king's daughter. Seduction ap-
> pears in my book as women's silk petticoats hanging in a
> shop window. The words through which I express the effect
> of it on my hungry hero are: "Perfume of embraces all him
> assailed. With hungered flesh obscurely, he mutely craved
> to adore."[2]

Other passages are more obviously and playfully homeric. Take
for example the broadly cannibalistic reflection elicited by the ar-
ray of food at Davy Byrne's "moral pub": "Ham and his descen-
dants mustered and bred there. Potted meats. What is a home
without Plumtree's potted meat? Incomplete . . . Under the obit-
uary notices they stuck it . . . Dignam's potted meat"—and so on
with gusto. The homeric allusions in passages like these may be
overlooked by the reader upon whose consciousness they are working, but the whimsy and the joy underlying their invention will
not. Since they do not correspond directly or exclusively to anything homeric, but only to Joyce's idiosyncratic reading of Homer
from a modern perspective, they do not detract from the organic
unity of the book.

Already by "Proteus,"[3] Joyce's third chapter, we are aware that he has shaped his novel less in terms of the analogy than of the situations of his major protagonists. Homer's poem recounts Telemachus' visit to Menelaus' palace where the aging hero tells the tale of his return from Troy, emphasizing his struggle with the sea god Proteus, who, once stilled, loses his power to change shape and must tell his conqueror how to escape from the island of Pharos. The god's nature impregnates Joyce's chapter where Stephen becomes the focal figure, a sort of combination of Menelaus on Pharos, Telemachus as his guest in Sparta, and, by virtue of the uneasy flux of his mind, Proteus himself. Most of the original action is conveyed analogically, but everything is displaced in favor of Stephen's identity crisis, which is in itself a projection of the problem of a fatherless Telemachus searching for his function. (Actually Stephen is trying to shed Telemachus' duties in order to exercise those of the free spirit.)

In the central chapters Joyce goes much further. The order of the episodes is rudely shifted. "Nausikaa" follows "Cyclops" rather than (as in Homer) "Calypso." While Ulysses tells the tale of his travels to the Phaeacians (his narrative taking up most of the central portion), Bloom confines himself to a three-line recapitulation in "Nausikaa": "Long day I've had. Martha, the bath, funeral, house of keys, museum with those goddesses, Dedalus' song. Then that bawler in Barney Kiernan's. Got my own back there" (380). Joyce's "Hades" follows his "Lestrygonians" rather than (again as in Homer) "Circe." "Wandering Rocks," missing from Homer's account, is inserted as a pivotal chapter. Stephen-Telemachus' voyage dovetails with Bloom-Ulysses' travels. The fantasia in Circe's den, which falls so early in Homer's version, closes the central section and provides the book with its major dramatic climax, bodying forth an inferno more terrible than anything in "Hades." Joyce's innovations are even more obvious in the "Nostos," where Homer's unwieldly but suspense-and-action-packed return chapters are condensed into three virtually static episodes and the last word rises voluminous from the recumbent, unfaithful, and impatient Molly, the secret of whose jingling bed Bloom-Ulysses does not know.

Stuart Gilbert points out that Joyce had good reasons for choosing the half-piratical warrior chieftain as his parallel and a Jew as his protagonist.[4] Dublins' founding fathers were, after all, sea rovers too, and the earliest invaders and colonists are thought to have come from Greece or Scythia. One of Joyce's sources, Victor Bérard's *Les Phéniciens et l'Odyssée,* insists that Homer derived his travel narrative from the tales spun by Phoenician traders, Semites like Bloom. Ireland is in many ways similar to Greece, though the situation of the Irish in our times resembles that of the Jews in Roman times.

The justification may be elaborated much further, as indeed Joyce did in his rough notes, but of course Leopold Bloom is not Ulysses. He is rather the type of Ulysses, a latter-day exemplar isolated from wife and family by death and emotional distance. Neither is he heroic. He is hard put to cope even with the troubles of the little man in a modern, turbulent city. Stephen is not (like Telemachus) a fatherless Greek Ephebe who sheds his fears when he sails out into the big world. Instead he is a gifted but rather confused and dreamy Irish youth, unwashed, uncourageous, with frustrated ambitions. Yet, like Telemachus, he must somehow be grounded in reality before he can hope to achieve anything.

In each case the analogy is ironical and the irony cuts two ways to establish a fresh relationship and new attitudes toward the givens of both narratives. If Bloom is analogous to Ulysses, and we can point not only to their parallel adventures but to traits that they share, then Bloom is ennobled by the conjunction with the hero. But since he falls so far short in his nature and behavior and in the quality of his adventures, we must also see him as diminished by the relationship, a grotesque shadow of the heroic precursor. The two attitudes generated by Joyce's metaphor, though virtually opposite, do not negate each other. Instead, they set up a fruitful tension within our conception of the chapter and revitalize our hackneyed view of the heroic prototype.

Joyce's ironic re-vision of the classic text is subtle and pervasive. As part of a hardening and polishing process, Homer's Athena sends the callow Telemachus to visit Nestor, the king of horse-rich Pylos, before she sends him to the warrior prince, Menelaus. Nestor is a gentle, pious, fatherly sort who will be tolerant of the boy's awkwardness. As it happens, Telemachus does astonishingly well, impresses the wise old man with his bearing and tact, and participates in a sacrifice before being sent on his way with good advice. In *Ulysses* the allusions to this event and the parallels are numerous and specific, and neither Nestor-Deasy's experience nor Stephen's callowness is in question. But Joyce's Telemachus is a teacher as well as a pupil, and though he listens patiently enough, he is embarrassed, and galled by the old man's preachments. It is ironic, given Stephen's antinationalist sentiments, that Deasy links him to the Fenians and, given his artistic credo, that he identifies him with journalism. It is more ironic that the old Orangeman's opinions provoke reactions that underline Stephen's failure to sever the ties that bind him to Ireland and Irish causes. Despite himself, Stephen cannot join the horse-fancying Orangeman in an attack on his own freely rejected church and party. His is still the not invalid Catholic position that the Protestant establishment has camped on the prostrate body of the majority. Unlike Telemachus, the Ithacan bumpkin, who is overawed by the splendor of the rich king's facilities, Stephen is unimpressed by Deasy's connections, his possessions, and his "wisdom." Unlike the generous Nestor, Deasy is a provincial, free with advice but lacking in respect for Stephen's forefathers and stingy with his money. Still Deasy is no more a simple caricature of Nestor than Stephen is of Telemachus. (After all, Homer's "tamer of horses" is of remarkably little help to his visitor, who must in the end rely on his own powers.) Both are freely adapted and ironically conceived projections whose relationships to the Greek originals are strikingly similar to Stephen's relationship to Bloom.

The freedom with which Joyce adapted his sources can be seen also in the expansion of a minor episode like the perilous voyage between the rock Scylla and the whirlpool Charybdis. Here he elaborated a splendid conceit, letting the spartan life in Stratford stand for the rock while the whirlpool is symbolized by Plato, syncretistic mysticism, and the profuse life of London. He presents John Eglinton (the dogmatic country boy who champions Aristotle) and AE (the theosophical aesthete and platonist) as the poles between which Stephen hangs his argument, bending this way or that to mollify and please the opponents he wishes to woo. Inevitably Stephen is caught in both traps, from which Mulligan's wit unpleasantly extricates him. Bloom, who enters the library in time to see Stephen rent and submerged, is untouched by learning and reason. Like Ulysses, he passes through unscathed, though he is already drawn to Stephen as surrogate son (if not as a lost crew member). The danger has of course been ludicrously minimal. But Joyce was not content with this; he felt the need to expose Bloom further. Accordingly, he ended his chapter by having him sail through the library portals between the whirlpool of irony (Stephen) and the rock of mockery and malice (Mulligan), a genuine escape if a comic one.

Other Analogies

The *Odyssey* analogies are the most carefully elaborated of Joyce's allusions, but the others, while less pronounced, are by no means gratuitous. Though there is no reason to maintain in so rich a context a constant awareness of subidentities which are only periodically underlined, we take pleasure in the sudden discovery of a subtly stated parallel and the consequent enlargement of the being of one of the protagonists and the frame of the book. Bloom-Ulysses-Shakespeare-Dante-Ahazuerus-St. Anthony-God-etcetera and the Stephen-Telemachus-Hamlet-Shakespeare-Icarus-Daedalus-Faust-Wandering Aengus-Christ-etcetera do not exist as cluster characters but rather as single and singular personages sharing with their models certain distinguishing traits and oscillating between and among the possibilities thus suggested.

There may be no hard and fast rule for the "identifications," but we note that frequently they come in antagonistic pairs, sometimes in unified groups of three (Telemachus, Ulysses, Penelope; Hamlet, Shakespeare, Ann Hathaway); often they attract a whole body of subsidiary relationships (see for example the way the Hamlet analogy invites us to identify Deasy with Polonius or Mulligan and Haines with Rosencrantz and Guildenstern).[5] At times they are actually part of the character's view of himself or others. Thus, in a Byronic mood, Stephen sees himself as the fallen Lucifer or Icarus while under other auspices he identifies with a betrayed Christ or an accomplished Daedalus. The hints are there, the substructure has been carefully elaborated, but, as we may recall, few noticed even the most obvious of the analogies until Stuart Gilbert published his study.

Though Joyce told Frank Budgen that Faust, as opposed to the many-sided Ulysses, is rootless, "no-aged," and incomplete,[6] Goethe's *Faust* was one of the earliest correlatives for *Ulysses*. As early as 1907, Joyce explained to his brother Stanislaus that his novel "would depict an Irish Faust, heroic and full of presumption." As Richard Ellmann remarks, he had probably begun to think of the book as autobiographical.[7] Yet, while it is a critical commonplace that Joyce patterned "Circe" after the famous witches' sabbath, or *Walpurgisnacht,* it is not widely recognized that he used the analogy elsewhere. We do not need his comments to discover similarities between Faust and Stephen as romantic overreachers. Having devoted a lifetime to seeking union with the absolute through study and teaching, Faust discovers that he has earned only fatigue and disillusionment. In his tomblike study he turns to magic books, hoping to gain illegitimately what he could not achieve by legitimate (sanctified or scholastic) means. After his failure with the Earth Spirit, who rejects him as a half-man living only in his mind, he contemplates suicide before capitulating to Mephistopheles, who restores his youth and permits him to complete his identity. Stephen's case is both strikingly similar and remarkably different. Having cultivated only one side of his being and nourished himself on dead learning "coffined thoughts . . . in mummycases, embalmed in spice of words" (193), he too lives among shriveled hopes in a kind of cell (see the tower and his mind). He too acts the teacher unconvinced by his teaching, contemplates suicide, meditates on the purpose of life, recognizes but is frustrated by the need for change, and fears the fall from grace. Though we can understand his disillusionment, there is something absurd about Stephen's self-involvement, his love of abstruse lore, his inability to shed the chains of a religion to which he no longer feels committed, his perverse asceticism. It seems inappropriate for so young a man to be so crabbed and aged, so sober even when drunk, so intense. Yet these are all temporary Faustian traits which combine with a permanent Faustian inner energy and drive. For the rest, that merry devil Mulligan does his living for him, and provides a model and a goad he distrusts, fears, and envies.

The *Faust* themes coalesce towards the end of "Circe" where, reversing Faust's development, the witch's magic turns Stephen momentarily from a boy into an old man:[8] *"His features grow drawn and grey and old"* (582). The moment is particularly Faustian, following as it does the dance with a whorewitch and the vision of a *"green crab with malignant red eyes"* emanating from the ghost of his mother, who doubles in this context as the innocent Gretchen whom Faust got with child. This is a conflation of details from several incidents. In *Faust* a red mouse emerges from the mouth of the naked young witch with whom the old-young man is dancing, and Gretchen is seen as dead but still intact, a warning of her impending execution for infanticide. Faust's reaction is one of passionate sympathy and repentance for having left her to this fate. Stephen rebels, breaks from the memory in terror and disgust. His need is to rid himself of the "agenbite of inwit" (remorse of conscience) rather than to enlarge upon it.

A less dramatic and more typical example is Stephen's second appearance in "Wandering Rocks," where the context more than justifies references to the scholar-magician, whose frustration at the beginning of Goethe's play-book parallels the young man's claustrophobia. Here Stephen wanders aimlessly from a jeweler's window to a bookseller cart where he contemplates an odd assortment of books and meets his sister Dilly. Superficially, there are no parallels for this action in *Faust*. (Stephen's graphic vision of death by drowning and his confession of guilt remind one more of *Hamlet*.) The lapidary's unburied treasure, however, recalls fallen angels and brings on visions of hellish terrors and Circean ("swinish") oriental delights. In the larger context it also suggests Mephisto's method of supplying Faust with wealth. Stephen becomes more specifically Faustian when he muses unhappily on his kinship with the gem-polishing jeweler, a creature from a lower world: "Grandfather ape gloating on a stolen hoard. And you who wrest old images from the burial earth! The brainsick words of sophists: Antisthenes. A lore of drugs" (242). Like Faust he is aware that his knowledge is corrupt, little better than the "base treasure of a bog" (29) he noticed in Deasy's office. At his next stop, the dusty bookcart with its load of dead learning, Stephen finds a book with magical spells by an abbot, Peter Salanka, whom he mockingly equates with his own favorite, Joachim de Flora. It is from this sort of text that Goethe's hero extracts the spells that raise the devil. The murmured spell ("—*Se el yilo nebrakada femin-*

inum!'' [242]) brings Dilly, whom Stephen pictures by the fire in a vignette that may recall the famous "Witches' Kitchen" scene: "It glowed as she crouched feeding the fire with broken boots" (243). This is the moment of Faust's magical transformation into a youth, during a scene which features, along with the witch and her sire, the witch's apes and the mirror in which Faust sees the reflection of his ideal. Like her mother in "Circe," Dilly does double duty, suggesting both witch and Gretchen and more. She also functions as his mirror: "My eyes they say she has. Do others see me so? Quick, far and daring. Shadow of my mind." Ironically, her eyes give him back no inspiration, no light, only deep despair and the vision of her-him drowning in "Misery! Misery!" (243).

Telemachus and Faust are among the exceptions to the rule that Stephen supplies his own subidentities. Bloom's identities, in accordance with Joyce's more light-hearted conception of him, and apart from the *Odyssey* framework, are generally evolved by others. Stephen works out the motivation and condition of Shakespeare, which we in our turn apply to Bloom's situation as a mastered and cuckolded husband, and a father whose dead son would now be about eleven, the age when Hamnet Shakespeare died. Goaded by Eglinton, Stephen goes so far as to find "Jewish" traits in the playwright, traits which Bloom ironically enough lacks. For the most part, the plodding, tasteless Dublin Jew is Shakespeare in contradistinction to as well as in terms of Stephen's definition. Yet, when Stephen concludes his argument with something resembling a creator's credo, we suddenly discover striking, pointed, and even plausible relationships between Shakespeare as artist-God, God the creator, and Leopold Bloom, the former employee of a slaughter house and the husband who implicitly offers his wife to others:

> . . . the lord of things as they are whom the most Roman of catholics call *dio boia*, hangman god, is doubtless all in all in all of us, ostler and butcher, and would be bawd and cuckold too but that in the economy of heaven, foretold by Hamlet, there are no more marriages, glorified man, an androgynous angel, being a wife unto himself. (213)

In *Ulysses,* more emphatically than Stephen or any other character, Bloom is the "lord of things as they are," not only in the sense that he is supremely aware of pragmatic reality but also in Stephen's

Aristotelian sense that his soul, or "form of forms," incorporates more, since it apprehends more of Dublin than any other soul in the book. (In a jocular vein Bloom's masturbation fulfills the prediction in the last phrase of the citation.)

Joyce scatters other identities for Bloom broadcast through the novel. He lets Mulligan, for example, identify him with the Wandering Jew in "Scylla" and suggests, through Stephen in "Proteus," a Moses identity. He links Bloom to Elijah, whose return will announce the Last Judgment and the Second Coming, through the throwaway he tosses into the river Liffey, through the concluding commentary in "Cyclops," and through juxtaposition in the conclusion to "Oxen of the Sun." As a projection of Jehovah, Bloom gathers up the fallen Stephen, a projection of the slain Christ, and with the aid of death's representative Corny Kelleher protects him from the watch so that he may escort him to the abode of bliss. (Such parallels are confirmed, or rather reaffirmed, in the most hilarious manner during "Circe," where Bloom takes on a whole constellation of further but clearly spurious identities and even becomes momentarily feminine.) One suspects that Bloom as law giver and messiah would be far better than the citizen but little better than his own hallucinated persona in "Circe," where he proclaims the "new Bloomusalem in the Nova Hibernia of the future" (484) and announces his version of the Ten Commandments:

> Union of all, jew, moslem and gentile. Three acres and a cow for all children of nature. Saloon motor hearses. Compulsory manual labour for all. All parts open to the public day and night. Electric dish-scrubbers. Tuberculosis, lunacy, war and mendicancy must now cease. General amnesty, weekly carnival, with masked licence, bonuses for all, esperanto the universal brotherhood. No more patriotism of bar-spongers and dropsical impostors. Free money, free love and a free lay church in a free lay state. (489–90)

In mocking Bloom here, Joyce mocks as well the aspirations of Jews and Irish alike, for both desire an impossible earthly kingdom. It is not always clear how we should take these and other identifications, but surely most of them are absurd and grotesque in ways that the *Odyssey* and Shakespeare parallels are not. Possibly Joyce had set out to undermine most emphatically the grave aspects of this book which are associated with Stephen and his fate, by re-projecting his other-worldly concerns in terms of a clownish emblem of humanity whose virtues outweigh his faults but hardly merit such stiff-necked seriousness. Stephen, as he is presented to us in *Ulysses*, is imbued with the sort of fanaticism and dogmatism which characterized the Jews in ancient times. Bloom, despite his inadequacies, is characteristically easy going, delighting in his humanity, and delighted by the world and the flesh. For him the world of the spirit, "that other world," is simply a typing error in a coy letter (77).

In this connection we have an identification for Bloom that corresponds to the Faust identity for Stephen, namely with Flaubert's ascetic hermit Saint Anthony. The hero of *La Tentation de St. Antoine*[9] is a proper response to the romantic overreacher in *Faust*. Both works have contributed (perhaps with some side glances at Dante) to the form of Joyce's "Circe," which, like them, is written as a play and which combines and blends their attributes. If in that chapter Stephen's experiences follow those of the peripatetic Faust whose comic devil (see Lynch in "Circe" and Mulligan elsewhere) is partly a projection of his psychic need, Bloom experiences the hallucinatory frenzy of an immobile Saint Antoine, whose visions reconstitute in a disorderly fashion his past and embody his repressed desires in like profusion. The worldly but curiously abstemious, isolated, and naïve Bloom is ironically cast as the self-tormenting saint, who has rejected the world only to find it within his own nature. The unworldly and ascetic Stephen, who has been thrown in the middle of the action to which he has yet to adjust, is both appropriate and anomalous in the Faustian role of a scholar-hero who rejects explicitly the sort of life Stephen is leading between pubs, libraries, and student carouses.

The Shakespeare-Hamlet framework is appropriate to the themes of fatherhood, exile and estrangement, adultery, death, divinity, and creativity, which constitute the bulk of Joyce's thematic concerns. The Faust and Saint Antoine framework can accommodate a number of others. But since it is not stated as a theme but rather made to contribute directly to the form, and hence available like the *Odyssey* but lower on the scale of values, it functions principally as a means of corroborating the larger development of the day, paralleling the drift of Stephen and Bloom toward self-fulfillment and resignation. Just as Stephen and Bloom momentarily combine to make a complete man who might resemble Shakespeare and contribute to a shakespearian trinity, the *Walpurgisnacht* in which Faust recognizes the depths to which he has sunk and Saint Antoine's night of tormenting self-discovery and disillusionment combine to create the drama of disclosure which inverts the daytime identities of Stephen and Bloom and permits them to achieve spiritual unity.

Clowns and clowning constitute yet another sort of mesh in Joyce's analogical net, one which joins the two principal character groups in a vital but distinctly conventional formal union and at the same time engages us in a new thematic and structural complex. The clown figure is introduced emphatically on page one with the prancing, prating, mocking Buck Mulligan, the jester of the Irish literary revival, a figure whose type conforms to the conventional pantomime and *Commedia dell' Arte* figure of mirth and mischief, Harlequin. Mulligan and Boylan constitute a pair; Bloom and Stephen, as their somber and ill-favored counterparts, each function as a projection of the sad clown, Pierrot. Molly, in obvious conjunction with the pastoral Gerty and possibly also with Stephen's fickle muse, is identifiable as Columbine.

While Bloom and Boylan are clearly clowns by nature on the stage of life, Stephen and Mulligan consciously hide behind the mask created by literary predecessors. If Buck is the most polished performer, Bloom is the most versatile clown, and the most engaging. His apotheosis in "Circe," coming after we have discerned in chapter after chapter traces of the gently ridiculous, is a farrago of traditions and techniques disclosing the accomplished mime, the fool of many faces whose strength lies in his display of weakness. Unconsciously, he becomes the most conventional sort of performer, projecting in a number of guises mock mastery and endearing humiliation. By contrast, Stephen, who has to his own mind played the jester while teaching, disputing, or prating grave nonsense, becomes in "Circe" the frenetic puppet, a pathetic version of Mulligan (19), "with shrugged shoulders, finny hands outspread, a painted smile on his face'' (569) before rushing madly to a mock-destruction reminiscent of the fate of so many post-Romantic Pierrots. It is consistent with Joyce's method that the farcical "Circe," where comic stereotypes are dominant, is the most serious of the book's chapters, the one that exposes and cleanses, for the moment at least, the deepest wounds. Here we are far nearer the truth of Stephen's dilemma than we are in either "Proteus," where Stephen is masked against himself, or "Scylla," where he is armed against others. Likewise Bloom, in acting out in sequence the most degrading roles, has reached a bottom from which he can only rise.

If we bear in mind their existence and are not distracted by their subtle glow, the analogies have many practical functions. Through them, the characters can complete not one but many actions, live many lives, resume history, achieve heroic or divine stature. They can be united metaphorically or be made to conform to the structures of various logical systems. Since these are no more than analogies, no such identification need in fact occur and the realistic "curve" is maintained. Through them also the logic of time and place is distorted, and we achieve a sense of the universal as a component of a statement of particularity. This is not the case in Joyce's next book, which, in accordance with his practice, reverses the concerns of *Ulysses* and places the analogical identities first, letting us pierce through an awareness of the "omnibody" ("Here Comes Everybody") to a sense of the modest individual who is nobody in particular.

The Strongest Irony

"Pooh!" says the Wilde-like dandy Mulligan, "We have grown out of Wilde and paradoxes. It is quite simple. He proves by algebra that Hamlet's grandson is Shakespeare's grandfather and that he himself is the ghost of his own father" (18). Joyce never goes quite this far, but he does base his book in paradox. This is probably inevitable in a book which combines a Platonic "symbolism" (a tendency to deal with man as a glass through which we glimpse a higher or at least more universal reality) with an Aristotelian "realism" (a tendency to treat existence as an opaque fact).

One thinks of Joyce's favorite heretic, Giordano Bruno (1548–1600), the philosopher of Nola, who insisted that opposites are identical, that the greatest is equivalent to the least, the longest to the shortest, the coldest to the hottest, the finite to the infinite, and who, centuries before Leibnitz, generated out of apparent disharmony the real harmony of the world.[10] Whatever its merits as philosophy, this principle, which appropriately contradicts without completely invalidating the Aristotelian bases for the book, served Joyce well in *Ulysses,* where he pitted every aspect against not one but several opposite equivalents, and where unity is found through the vital instability of these relationships.

The bright cloudless day through which men wander blind to their needs and harried by their aspirations is seen in relation to the evening and night where they find enlightenment and discover themselves in their hidden nature. The un-Irish Bloom is equated with and set against the city which rejects him. Stephen is paradoxically identified with a man who is in every apparent sense his antitype. The analogical systems, each of which is based on paradoxical relationships, clash when they are juxtaposed. How do we go about identifying Ulysses' travels, the Passion of Christ, and Shakespeare's life? Structural elements are pitted against passages that set them in fresh ironic light. "Cyclops," with its discordant male voices, its medley of styles, its low narrator and comic Irish spirit, and its concluding catastrophe, is echoed in "Oxen of the Sun," where the contrived wit of the carousers is recounted in grave and elevated styles and the whole crew is flushed out into the night along with Mina Purefoy's afterbirth. It is essential that we compare and even equate the two circumstances, though they too are extremes, being on the one hand the expression of wasted lives through spontaneous folk wit and on the other of youthful potential wasted through the labored wit of intellectuals. Joyce makes this point when he shows Bloom to be for opposite reasons an outsider at both gatherings.

Paradox is also the hallmark of Stephen's conversation and thought, but not of his alone. In "Scylla and Charybdis," one of Wilde's gravest and most incriminating paradoxes (his theory that Shakespeare's sonnets were written for one Willie Hughes) is humorlessly defended by the Quaker Lyster: "Do you think it is only a paradox . . . The mocker is never taken seriously when he is most serious" (109). On which Stephen, paradoxically assuming Mulligan's role as mocking chronicler of Dublin's literati, reflects, "They talked seriously of mocker's seriousness." For Joyce, who left Ireland so that he could create his country out of himself, paradox is generally both real and apparent, like the frequent incongruous-seeming juxtapositions and the idea of taking as his model for the all-city the down-at-the-heel capital of a subject province imbued with a sense of its glorious past and characterized by its dormant potential. But real and apparent paradoxes have always been the stock-in-trade of religious thinkers, mystics, and poets, and, as Joyce repeatedly suggests, Jerusalem in Christ's time was an eastern Dublin, smarting under the heel of Rome.

Like just about every other aspect of *Ulysses*, paradox is both a method and theme, contributing to stasis and motion. Seen as negation, that is, as a cancelling out of one item by its contrary, it is equivalent to paralysis, another of Joyce's favorite themes and a term applied to the Dublin of *Dubliners*. The idea of the dropsical ruin of a "citizen" leading a revolution is a case in point, as is the view of Ireland hoping to win the status of a new power by turning back the clock. On the other hand, we have the portrait of a Bloom, complete from dandruff to piles, as the norm for humanity, or we have Stephen sharing and systematically reversing the thoughts of his antitype. In these instances, despite apparent absurdities, neither term of the paradox is cancelled out, though both are altered to good effect, and a dynamic balance is achieved. We can point also to the medial nature of Bloom's attributes and to the fact that, without identifying with him, we sense repeatedly that he is doing and feeling as we might. Hence the further paradox that we find ourselves attuned against our will to the nature of the undistinguished failure. This is the sort of reaction that a satirist might hope to inspire, but Joyce's book is only marginally satirical.

The parallelism of Stephen's thought with Bloom's is more than the product of novelistic license which permits coincidence, if not opposite equivalence, as a structural device. Their paired reflections do more than emphasize their complementary dispositions. They produce a fruitful tension and a Janus-faced awareness which will be stored in our communal mind in readiness for the indiscriminate thought-texture of "Circe." In "Aeolus," Bloom, ever objective in his response but just recently returned from the funeral, watches the presses and reflects with gruesome logic on machines and men, conjoining with paradoxical effect organic and inorganic images:

> Machines. Smash a man to atoms if they got him caught. Rule the world today.[11] His machineries are pegging away too. Like these, got out of hand: fermenting. Working away, tearing away. And that old grey rat tearing to get in. (118)

There are echoes here from Stephen's ghastly projection in "Proteus" of the putrefying corpse of the drowned man, whose fate calls to mind nature's economy (50). But more powerful echoes occur in "Wandering Rocks," where a cosmic catastrophe is generated in Stephen's mind by the sight of Old Russell at his lapidary wheel and the sound of "dynamos from the powerhouse":

> Beingless beings. Stop! Throb always without you and the throb always within. Your heart you sing of. I between them. Where? Between two roaring worlds where they swirl, I. Shatter them, one and both. But stun myself too in the blow. Shatter me you who can. (242)

Images, ideas, and impulses are parallel. Both men accommodate the circumstances to their concerns and personalities, but Bloom has rendered the machines as organisms while Stephen has turned from machine and organism to the cosmos. Bloom is engaged by a world that Stephen is determined to turn into a metaphor. Stephen's "roaring worlds" are mental and personal; Bloom's interacting gears are physical and impersonal. Both men are aware of the impulse to dominate and both are repulsed by force, but Bloom masters his fear by capitulating to it while Stephen increases his terror by pretending to meet force with force. Even the sense of motion is opposite. Bloom sees piston action and rasping, while Stephen sees and feels rotation and collision. Two very different minds, moved by a similar stimulus and expressing their concerns in opposite ways, become ironically identified in our minds while remaining distinct and unreconcilable.

Joyce's rigorous use of apparent paradox is a major source of *Ulysses'* charm, as is its quality as a self-perpetuating puzzle, a portable infinity symbol. It is also a source of exasperation for readers eager to conclude, for though it can readily vitalize even the most trivial event, thought, or identity, it will not fix or define, and it acts as a solvent for conclusions. Thus, in terms of his realistic context, Joyce is playing an interesting double game. On the one hand, he does everything he can to render immediate the circumstances of his Dublin world, to engross us in the fates of his protagonists. We are almost as eager to see things turn out well on June 16 as we are to see the hero of melodrama succeed or fail. After all, we have invested much time and emotion in the protagonists' natures. But Joyce obliges us to see them from a distance, even when we are engaged by their minds. He constantly opposes them to more attractive characters or exposes them in repulsive or unpleasant acts or juxtaposes them so that they expose each other or suggests absurdly appropriate analogies.

To Not Conclude

Where does this leave us at the end of the day? Certainly, Stephen will not always be a young man or an irresolute one. On the other hand, he probably will not establish any sort of liaison with Molly or function as a replacement for Bloom's lost son. Still, we may question the impact of the two sorts of violence in "Circe," the inner and the outer, the degree of Stephen's liberation from the tendencies not of a day but of a lifetime, and the significance of the meeting with Bloom. Is the positive act of refusing Bloom's offer a sign that Stephen has been altered? It is certainly the first and only decision he comes to, though his motives are obscured by the chapter's technique. As for Bloom, the degradation he experiences with mixed bliss and horror in "Circe" will not work any permanent miracle, or even measurably increase his self-awareness, though it seems to have rendered possible and plausible his behavior in the rest of the book. His dream of a future association with Stephen is on a level with his travel plans and his literary ambitions. His cuckolding is confirmed and silently accepted. As a result of his request for breakfast in bed, Molly lets her thoughts drift back to a relationship she has taken for granted and contemplates a gross seduction consonant with the "Circe" visions before she mellows into her reaffirmation of their romance. All of this has a nice conclusive ring, but what does it mean?

Joyce's chapters, most particularly the nocturnal ones, are full of "turning points," lesser moments of decision and recognition, but then every instant is both a moment of change and a continuation of the unbroken process of identity, the actualization of the possible. This is what Stephen means when, drunken and out of sorts, he reacts to Lynch's mocking reference to Bruno[12] by paraphrasing Maeterlinck:[13]

> What went forth to the ends of the world to traverse not itself. God, the sun, Shakespeare, a commercial traveller, having itself traversed in reality itself, becomes that self . . . Self which it itself was ineluctably preconditioned to become. (505)[14]

Though perhaps too solipsistic, this view suggests the sort of process underlined both by the paradoxes and analogies and by the treatment of action in *Ulysses*. (It also motivates Stephen's despair by ruling out choice and obviating decision.) Under the circumstances, it would require extraordinary ingenuity to define unequivocally Joyce's attitude toward an event or to establish anything as crucial. Yet the question will bear a closer look.

Two recent critics draw consolation from "Ithaca." Returning to his bed, Bloom finds in his place "the imprint of a human form, male, not his, some crumbs, some flakes of potted meat, recooked, which he removed" (731). The laconic catechist proceeds to expose Bloom's reactions beginning with his smile at the thought of the twenty-four oddly assorted males whom he imagines to have preceded Boylan and then analysing his "antagonistic sentiments": "Envy, jealousy, abnegation, equanimity" (732). For Arnold Goldman, the sequence suggests that Bloom has graduated from the Kierkegaardian "ethical" phase to his "religious"

deal of liquid, but since he has previously been less than warm if
not quite cold, we may read his "suggestion" as a mildly friendly
overture, a sign of gratitude or, as Hart suggests, a "recognition
of common humanity."[21] Joyce has deliberately and comically be-
fogged the issue by first having the two men stand silently, "each
contemplating the other in both mirrors of the reciprocal flesh of
theirhisnothis fellowfaces" (702). This is a moment of equivocal
recognition, but it seems to dissolve the joined reflection in
"Circe." Then there is the micturition itself, described with the
usual comic precision and accompanied by thoughts that have little
to do with a meeting of minds. Rather they could suggest a severance and emphasize a distance which has never been bridged.
Bloom is thinking self-consciously of the qualities of his organ
while Stephen is reflecting on circumcision as a probable consequence of Bloom's Jewishness but, characteristically (and comically), in terms of the religious significance of Christ's foreskin:
". . . the carnal bridal ring of the holy Roman catholic apostolic
church, conserved in Calcata . . ." (703). We may be pleased to
note that Stephen is thinking of someone other than himself, but
we should not push that point too far, for he is treating and has
treated Bloom as a source of information, and besides Joyce has
another paradox at hand. According to the clearest statement on
the subject, Bloom is uncircumcised (373), but since the two men
circumspectly shield their members, Stephen cannot know this.
Union? Communion? Understanding? Equanimity? In the absence of answers it is best not to conclude or to conclude in a variety of ways on various levels of the experience while keeping the
analogies in mind as patterns for unrealized possibilities.

Perhaps this is what Joyce is suggesting when he defines the
*wake*ing world of the dreamer of *Finnegans Wake* (who may be identical with the reader) as a "collideorscape," a kaleidoscopic landscape full of collisions and escapes. If so, we may approach the
joycean universe armed with a sort of permutation theory. Since
the world of each individual is subject to a great many but not an
infinitude of change, patterns will in the natural course of events
repeat themselves, but since the moment is conditioned by those
that precede or follow it, history "repeats itself with a difference."

Thus a crucified Christ rejects paradise, the prodigal son rejects the father he has sought, and, as Joyce puts it in one of his notes, Ulysses is unlucky, Penelope is unfaithful. Whether we extend the metaphor to include mankind or apply it to a single individual (as for example Stephen, with whose pattern we are familiar from the *Portrait*), universals may be said to underlie all particulars and the least little act reverberates in history if not in the stars. In this perspective there can be no end, no solution, no resolution—only illusory fixes in which the components, like the bits and pieces of colored glass or paper in a kaleidoscope, seem to compose themselves into meaningful patterns which of necessity vanish before we have grasped their integrity or deciphered their implications.

V

Form and Surface

Structural Strategies

No one denies that *Ulysses* is, for better or worse, a technical *tour de force* though some regret the lengths to which Joyce went in elaborating this quality. S. L. Goldberg goes further than most:

> In parts of "Cyclops" or "Nausicaa," "Eumaeus," or even "Ithaca," for example, the energy of the writing is largely destructive, and it is elaborated too willfully to sustain our interest once we have taken the comparatively simple point it is making.[1]

On the surface this position is valid. Certain chapters strain our patience, almost as much as the biblical "begats," working against the realistic context elaborated earlier, but we may ask if, in the total context, these are in fact flaws and if any aspect of *Ulysses* can be thought of as making a "simple point." Essentially, this is an attack on the later chapters, where Joyce abandons much of the paraphernalia of realism, but it includes as well a criticism of Joyce's self-indulgence (an unmeasurable quantity) and an attack aimed at the artist moving toward *Finnegans Wake* rather than the one moving from the *Portrait*. Such criticism suggests that a further step is necessary, an examination less of the much scrutinized devices as isolated phenomena than of the role of style and technique within a coherent structure, a look which could in its turn help illuminate other aspects of the book.

The time has passed when we could stop our consideration of

Joyce's strategy with a discussion of the "stream of consciousness" technique. This, though fascinating in its details and possibilities, was neither completely original with Joyce, nor uniform, nor even dominant in *Ulysses*. There is no real reason to doubt that, though he clearly perfected and enlarged the technique, Joyce derived it most directly from Edouard Dujardin's novelette *Les Lauriers sont coupés* (*We'll to the Woods no More*), a copy of which he bought in a station in 1903.[2] He used the technique as he did many others to do specific jobs, and principally, to bring into unusually sharp focus the alert conscious minds of individuals whose character he wished to define quickly, completely, and unmistakably before dissolving individuality and disclosing the basis of character in hidden impulses.

Neither can we stop with a consideration of the homeric justification for the specific techniques or, for that matter, with a tabulation of the rhetorical devices in "Aeolus," a list of the models for Joyce's pastiches in "Oxen of the Sun," or an account of his "musical techniques" in "Sirens." Treatments of such ingenious effects, though in themselves engrossing, are rather like the explanations of jokes. They give more pleasure to the speaker than to the listener. The *Odyssey* supplied more and less than an expendable scaffolding. Too many of Joyce's effects were dictated by the analogy for us to ignore the rationale for such rewarding effects as the windy rhetoric of "Aeolus," the impertinent use of the "fuga per canonem" in "Sirens," the "gigantism" of "Cyclops," or the chunks of irregularly shaped prose fashioned for "Wandering Rocks." Though on a second reading we may feel that Joyce labors some of his tricks, we would not care to ignore their role as part of a discrete and ironical backdrop. Still, given the freedom with which he interpreted his models and taking into consideration the density of *Ulysses,* these analogies do not suffice to justify his literary pyrotechnics, explain his choices, or illuminate the impact of the styles on the reader.

As an innovator, with a passion for pulling the technical stops, Joyce broke violently with tradition when he decided for whatever reason to evolve fresh styles for each of his chapters and thus systematically fragment his narrative. But his passion for freedom was easily, though not obviously, dominated by a rage for order.

This is reflected, to mention only a few of his controls, in the internal consistency of his chapters, in the graduated difficulty of his techniques, in the parallelism and interrelationship not only of characters, images, and analogies but even of chapter content, styles, and structures, and in the narrational strategy and the evolution of a nameless creative persona or "arranger." I use the term "arranger" to designate a figure or a presence that can be identified neither with the author nor with his narrators, but that exercises an increasing degree of overt control over increasingly challenging materials.

The early chapters modulate from a fairly conventional narrative, with stream of consciousness intrusions, toward the intricacies of Stephen's almost disembodied thought in "Proteus." From this we break into the lucid objectivity of Bloom's thought-stream in "Calypso." With Bloom, a latterday Brobdingnag, we enter the ordinary world through the door of the familiar rendered strange. From chapter to chapter, though not with predictable rigor, the dose of stylistic strangeness is increased, building toward and accumulating energy for the outrage of "Circe." After slogging through the viscosity of "Eumaeus" we enter a frigid "Ithaca," from which Molly's harsh but palpitating humanity is a welcome relief. "Penelope" completes a circle, being virtually unpunctuated and completely unmediated in imitation of liquid flow, the seemingly random musings of a satisfied woman between dreams on a hot spring night. To support this chronological development, Joyce systematically introduced ironic echoes and imposed through style and structure formal tensions which reflect back on the action, regulating its flux, broadening and illuminating its significance.

Just as the two protagonists' developments are analogous and interrelated, though antithetical and distinct, the chapters relating parallel phases of their developments are often structurally and even stylistically parallel. But this is not enough. A given chapter will invariably be related to several others by subject matter, complexity, imagery, and even by length. "Proteus," in which Stephen reflects unsystematically on his condition, taking his cues from a static landscape, must be related to "Scylla and Charybdis." There, reflecting systematically within an ambience made random by the conflicting voices, he constructs or rather redo not exhaust the stylistic play. Gerty's effusion reflects upon and balances "Penelope" to which it is the virginal response. It is also, like the Bloomish "literary" manner in "Eumaeus," a thoroughly artificial performance that conveys for all its evasiveness the quality of an experience. As for Bloom, it is altogether appropriate that he meditate in "Nausikaa" (as Molly does in "Penelope") on his own fleshcase. After all, at about this time Boylan is consummating his affair with the goddess of Bloom's dreams!

We find a similar constellation of chapters in "Scylla and Charybdis," "Cyclops," "Oxen of the Sun," and "Circe," all of which have elaborate overtones from the *Portrait*. The first three suggest, by virtue of their formats, symposia. All but "Oxen" are given near theatrical immediacy through style, though in each case the impact is as different as the narrative voice. All are carefully divided into acts and interludes. The second and third are full of parody and burlesque effects. Of course the parodies and burlesques in "Cyclops" are intrusive and unequivocally irreverent, though they tend to relate to as well as contrast with the action. Those in "Oxen" are organic but carefully shaded toward gravity in stark contrast to the tone of the proceedings. In "Cyclops," the most obvious humor is in the reaction; in "Oxen of the Sun," in the action. Similarly, "Scylla and Charybdis" shows the logical basis for the illogical action of "Circe," where Stephen's visions are perversely realized. Such interrelationships are as much an aspect of the arranger's role as the fact that both Bloom and Stephen are keyless this day; that Martha Clifford lives in Dolphin's Barn where Bloom courted Molly; that the Orangeman, Deasy, echoes the anti-Semitic sentiments of the proper Hibernophile Haines, while Mulligan shares attitudes with the all-Irish citizen.

Finally, there are the larger structural implications. The three chapters of the "Telemachia," for example, are reflected in the temporally coterminous opening chapters of the "Odyssey" section and in the "Nostos," which relates in its turn antithetically to the last three chapters of the central section. The central section, and hence the whole book, revolves around the eighteen plus one narrative fragments of "Wandering Rocks," a chapter unlike all the others in that it features Dublin rather than Bloom and Stephen and exposes the secret thoughts of four minor characters. It is more significant, however, that "Wandering Rocks" marks the beginning of the decline from daylight and social control into the license of the night, from the universe of clearly defined objects and ideas into the psychic space symbolized by two men urinating under the watchful stars and the soft-lit window of bedwarm Molly. The styles of the later chapters subtly mimic this development, providing an integral backdrop for the action and a commentary on it. Here balance is important. The night must not outweigh the day and the phases of the temporal and emotional journeys must have their appropriate weights (physical as well as rhetorical). A shorter or a more complex "Nausikaa" or a briefer and livelier "Ithaca" might spoil the "sit" of this coat of many colors.

When morning finally closes the night of *Finnegans Wake* and the dream identities seem to vanish, the narrator of the last chapter decrees that "every crisscouple [will] be so crosscomplimentary . . . in a farbiger pancosmos." But concerning the difference between the dream and waking worlds, he tells us, "Yet is no body present here which was not there before. Only is order othered. Nought is nulled."[3] The crisscrosscomplementary people of *Ulysses* have less far to travel than does the dream-reader of *Finnegans Wake*, but allowance made for the difference in scale, the same applies to the night world as opposed to the day world of Stephen and Bloom: "only is order othered." Joyce's problem was to suggest and enforce the impression of the interrelatedness and the opposition of the night and day consciousness, the unity of mankind and the uniqueness of individuals. The problem was a delicate one. On the one hand, he had to convey the multi-personal reality within the orderly frame of daily life in a large city. On the other, he wished to bring together under one hat his antitypes without doing violence to the logic of experience. He had already evolved ways of disclosing the nature of the individual. Here he would go further, exhibiting as well qualities that underlie and undercut individuality, the common substratum of historical and psychic experience. It is through the direct representation of subconscious urges in relation to an implied historical reality[4] that the "father" and the "son" will be identified and joined while being confirmed in their singularity.

In the *Portrait*, Joyce had to convey the quality of a developing mind and an evolving identity, to justify its evolution in terms of experience, to draw, that is, a true portrait. Since, in line with the traditions of flaubertian realism, he chose to write in an objective narrative voice (one through which the author's will is conveyed indirectly), he had to evolve styles which are mimic approximations of the mental rhythms of the growing boy, further justifications for his ultimate condition, and corollaries to the action. The problem was immensely more complex in *Ulysses* where space as well as time had to be dealt with and where he had to modulate from one sort of consciousness to another, from unity in diversity to diversity in unity. Like the distances travelled by Homer's heroes, the distances between day and night, outer and inner experience, Stephen and Bloom, the individual and the community, are incalculable. It was not a question of how to convey a natural process but rather how to combine without dilution contradictory modes. A physical and emotional impossibility had to be made plausible on a spiritual level.

To accomplish this Joyce contrived to develop *in extenso* the characters' daytime contexts, stressing the clarity of Stephen's thought and Bloom's observations before immersing both in a worldly context which he renders increasingly unrealistic and distant so that he can take us through and beyond the shadow play on the inner stage of the mind. In the later chapters Joyce's means seem to take over and the reader finds himself more obviously engaged by the esthetic surface which must ultimately serve not as a barrier but as a means of access to the drama within. Increasingly, he accepts a position halfway between the artist and his creation. As a creator engaged in the mechanics of the novel, he is capable of apprehending the vitality of the underlying order; as a spectator engaged by the characters' predicaments, he participates in their nature, from which he has been so carefully distanced. To understand and appreciate this minor miracle we must investigate the manipulation of the narrative voice, the evolving chapter techniques, and the intricacies of style on the level of the passage.

From Narrator to Arranger

Though we may be dazzled by the virtuosity of the artistic prime mover, we need not overlook a certain comforting consistency in the persona behind the action of the first eleven chapters. It is in small effects that his presence is first felt, in stylistic ticks or rather rhetorical gestures which add point, interest, and humor to what might otherwise be bland descriptive passages, connecting bits of dialogue or monologue. Quite apart from its content, each of the following brief citations has some locution in it that speaks for the narrator's particular brand of exuberance:

> He tore the flower gravely from its pinhold smelt its almost no smell. . . . (78)

The dead flower removed from Martha's letter during "Lotus Eaters" is endowed by the narrator with a comically poetic near-absence of smell. Again, the turn of phrase and the word choice set up a delightfully spurious tension. The overtones of violence in the act of tearing and in the "pinhold" are underscored by the adverb "gravely," which gives the action an absurdly funereal quality. We may compare the "almost no smell" to the "nocoloured eyes looking through the glass" of the sadistic Father Dolan in the *Portrait*.[5]

> Mr Bloom nodded gravely, looking in the quick bloodshot eyes. (105)

In keeping with the funeral context of "Hades," the narrator contrasts Bloom's *grave* nod with Mr. Kernan's "quick bloodshot eyes." A characteristic device is the double and perhaps triple reference of "gravely," which qualifies both verb and participle and rebounds against "quick," which is in turn qualified by "bloodshot." These eyes are quick with the life of the moribund, since, like Dignam, who died of drink, Kernan is a "lush."

> KYRIE ELEISON!
>
> A smile of light brightened his darkrimmed eyes, lengthened his long lips.
> —The Greek! he said again. *Kyrios!* Shining word! (133)

Here again are balanced opposites, in this case the components of Professor MacHugh's smile. The narrator's signature is on the "smile of light" which refers as much to the "shining" vowels of the Greek word as to the quality of MacHugh's expression. (Exceptionally, the headline seems to be both a summary of the action

and a part of the dialogue.) The smile exposes no teeth and the
light is confined to the eyes which are by contrast "darkrimmed."
The language almost cancels out the joy, and the light rhyme effects with which the sentence opens are weighted by the .heavy
Anglo-Saxon alliteration with which it ends. Not surprisingly, the
Greek is being compared to the Semite and Saxon. Though the
sentence's rhetorical density is appropriate to Stephen's thought
patterns and to the context ("Aeolus"), the narrator remains virtually identical with the speaker in the other pasages.

> Mr Best entered, tall, young, mild, light.
> He bore in his hand with grace a notebook, new, large,
> clean, bright. (186)

These two sentences from "Scylla and Charybdis" have the impact of a good pantomime sequence or a Beerbohm caricature.
More obtrusive than the earlier examples, they inevitably, if pleas-
antly, distract us from the dense fabric of the argument they inter-
rupt. The balanced strings of adjectives, the terminal rhymes, the
unpretentious monosyllables suggest the effort of a turn of the century schoolboy poet as well as the manners of a modern Ganymede
whose appearance gives Stephen his next irreverent point. Though
different in spirit from the other examples, these absurdly scan-
nable lines represent a mood of the narrator, the comic aside of
one who is capable of expressions like "turned an unoffending
face" or "repeated to John Elginton's newgathered frown" (187).

> By the stern stone hand of Grattan, bidding halt, an
> Inchicore tram unloaded straggling Highland soldiers of a
> band. (228)

Meter, alliteration, half-rhyme, and synecdoche contribute to the
rigid effect of Grattan's statue seen as a "stern stone hand" before
the sentence crumbles into flat-footed prose to imitate the movement of the "straggling Highland soldiers" only to close with a
lagging rhyme: "of a band."

> Bore this. Bored Bloom tambourined gently with I am
> just reflecting fingers on flat pad Pat brought. (279)

In "Sirens" the narrator loses ground. As in this sentence, his
voice is refined into "musical" prose complete with puns, facile

rhymes, alliteration, onomatopoeia. Though it is still recognizable as a vehicle capable of recording actual events and reactions, it is more audacious (see the "I am just reflecting fingers"), weaving together bits of overheard lyrics, thought fragments, and snatches of conversation to convey a total musical context. There is no fixed point of view.

After "Sirens" the narrator practically disappears, leaving behind a babble of voices but returning flittingly in Bloom's section of "Nausikaa" (379), or intruding occasionally in "Eumaeus," and more often in "Ithaca." In "Circe" Joyce reverses the naturalistic procedures by accurately describing illusions, or, as in the following passage, magically transforming tawdry nature:

> Rows of flimsy houses with gaping doors. Rare lamps with faint rainbow fans. Round Rabaiotti's halted ice gondola stunted men and women squabble. They grab wafers between which are wedged lumps of coal and copper snow. Sucking, they scatter slowly. Children. (429)

This description of houses with glowing fanlights and open doors on a dim-lit street is rendered more eerie by a speaker whose directions are meant to disorient us, who colors his details with words like "gaping," "faint," "stunted," "squabble" before he naturalizes the scene with a word: "Children." We have come a long way from the technique evident in the description of "two carfuls of tourists [which] passed slowly, their women sitting fore gripping frankly the handrests. Pale faces. Men's arms frankly round their stunted forms" (228). The "stunted forms" so succinctly presented by the narrator of "Wandering Rocks," whose point of view is momentarily Stephen's, are frankly incongruous, objects of open ridicule. In "Circe" the magical playwright speaks to us from our own point of view, and the creatures whom we are fooled into seeing as grotesques discomfort us as part of an unnatural landscape into which we are drawn by a web of illusion.

The narrator of the early chapters, with his marked concern for the word and its mutative powers and his relatively objective stance, operates as a brake on the very flux his language generates, if only because his voice is consistent. He also contributes a randomness of his own which foreshadows the intricate perspectival ambiguities of "Circe." A striking example of this is the following passage from "Telemachus," a telegraphic description of Mulligan dressing before Stephen, who reflects on what he sees:

> He emptied his pockets on to the table.
> —There's your snotrag, he said.
> And putting on his stiff collar and rebellious tie, he spoke to them, chiding them, and to his dangling watchchain. His hands plunged and rummaged in his trunk while he called for a clean handkerchief. Agenbite of inwit. God, we'll simply have to dress the character. I want puce gloves and green boots. Contradiction. Do I contradict myself? Very well then, I contradict myself. Mercurial Malachi. A limp black missile flew out of his talking hands.
> —And there's your Latin quarter hat, he said. (16–17)

There is no way of knowing what is said as opposed to what Stephen thinks of this dumb show sandwiched between the two presentations. Whether or not Buck speaks while his hands gesture is moot. The second half of the paragraph is a curious amalgam of possible and improbable utterance, some of which (like "Agenbite of inwit") is surely Stephen's, some of which may be remembered utterance, and again some, like the quotation from Whitman ("Do I contradict . . . myself"), may be a favorite tag. We have entered a dead space between thought and action, and, no matter how vivid the pantomime, we have a sense that the two individuals are momentarily and magically joined by the narrator whose procedures are more comprehensible on the thematic and analogical levels than on the mimetic. In this way he has foreshadowed the more emphatic miracle by which Bloom and Stephen are joined in Circe's looking-glass. By making a character address objects, by letting hands talk, a hat fly, a tie rebel, by creating, that is, out of the absurdities latent in our diction an enchanted landscape which we accept without question, he has also foreshadowed a more radical dislocation of reality. The muzziness in our citation is then deliberate. The narrator is obliging us to accept another order of reality. He is playing on our need to naturalize and explain the strange and elusive, to close the field of experience. He is also asserting his independence, his freedom from the rules he himself has established. Gradually and with calculated stealth this invisible but consistently locatable speaker will be metamorphosed into the artist-God as cosmic joker, the other side of Stephen's "hangman god." By the book's second half he will have become a creature of many faces but a single impulse, a larger version of his characters with a larger field of vision and many more perceptions to control, the figure I am calling the arranger.

The structural rhythm of the book, echoing and miming the "dance of the hours," is one of Joyce's most startling achievements and the greatest single justification for his style shifts. But the nature of this rhythm and the qualities that make it possible for Joyce to give coherence to a frame that can accommodate literary and psychic extremes can be understood only through a systematic study of Joyce's techniques for each chapter.

The Logic of Technique, the Dynamic of Arrangement

The first six chapters of *Ulysses* must be considered as a unit. They prepare the reader through dramatic exposition for the thematic concerns of the entire novel, through modifications in the techniques for the more radical style shifts of the later chapters, through the increasing use of the stream of consciousness for the phasing out of the conscious personal voice in the evening chapters. Stephen's point of view complemented by that of a sympathetic narrator dominates the first three chapters, Bloom's the next three. These chapters contain the clearest exposition and correspond to the four most clear-headed hours of the day.

"Telemachus" and "Hades" are social or group chapters which might be qualified as dramatic units. In contrast to the narrowly focussed *Portrait,* which it nevertheless continues, "Telemachus" presents each of its characters in a witty but objective light from a vantage point that is not necessarily Stephen's. Stephen's voice, which was first heard in the diary entries that conclude the *Portrait,* is here rendered as a secondary but more immediate commentary on action to which it is set in opposition and from which he feels excluded. His comments, concluding with the bitter "Usurper," are a source of unresolved tension. A secondary tension derives from the narrator's suggestive presentation through which a multitude of images and allusions manifest themselves. "Nestor" and "Lotus Eaters" present Stephen and Bloom in the center of a larger dramatic frame and give their voices and reactions clear precedence. In "Nestor" the narrator effaces himself in order to present everything through Stephen's eyes, acting more emphatically as a complement to his reactions. As a result, the other characters become as they have been in the *Portrait*, extensions of Stephen's experience, and Stephen stands suspended between young "ignorance" and old "wisdom" as a middle term. His stream of consciousness, in keeping with the educational setting, is so highly organized and rich in historical allusions that he seems to control the machinery of suggestion. "Proteus" and "Calypso" are the protagonists' most isolated performances. In "Proteus" the narrator's voice complements Stephen's self-conscious musings, making possible such effects as the Paris flashback and the visit to Uncle Richie. Stephen's voice, which at times blends inextricably with the narrator's, has become a protean instrument capable of a wide range of moods and effects, accurately reflecting his inner confusion but in a self-conscious and bookish style.

Like "Proteus," "Calypso" presents the character's (Bloom's) ambience in terms of his reactions. But here the narrator is a counterpersona. While Bloom reacts sardonically or humorously to aspects of his environment, the narrator is gently ironic about Bloom and through his treatment of details puts the Bloomish mentality into sharper relief. Bloom himself presents details with objective clarity in contrast to the subjective clarity of "Proteus." We are bombarded not with crystalline thought but with references to objects and actions each of which stands out against the field into which it will quickly blend. His thoughtstream, at once flexible and more natural, seems to have less inner coherence: a jumble of vivid and intimate details is thrown at us before we are properly introduced to our man.

"Lotus Eaters" puts Bloom in a more populous setting, permits him to react to more varied stimuli. Here, as in "Nestor," the narrator withdraws, becoming almost invisible, but returning occasionally to comment on details. In this, one of the more effective homeric chapters, the theme of torpid euphoria is echoed by the relaxed tone which mutes the eventful texture of the prose. Whereas in "Calypso" the narrator provided a comic counterpoint for Bloom's gentle humor, here Bloom is allowed to expose his own foibles while commenting on those of others. Two meetings (with M'Coy and Bantam Lyons) break the narrative, introducing voices that contrast with Bloom's, giving him a chance to comment within a more dynamic context.

The real contrast comes with "Hades" where Bloom's voice, though still dominant, is supplemented by dialogue. Here his humor becomes distinctly morbid and his voice increasingly subjective. The public and the private rhythms are boldly juxtaposed, and the narrator once more stands above the scene registering the action and moving out into the world so that other characters can comment on Bloom. Thus for the first time he introduces a secondary dramatic dimension. Bloom is a part of this scene in much the same way Stephen is a part of the action of "Telemachus,"[6] with this significant difference: Stephen is a grave and severely distanced protagonist, while Bloom is a comic character to whom we have begun to be attached.

In "Aeolus," the first chapter which Stephen and Bloom share, Joyce begins to undermine his narrative voice. The whimsical headlines assert a counter-nature to the objective persona, reminding us of the deliberate clowning in Sterne's *Tristram Shandy,* that early example of the self-shaping literary mind. Intrusive but not disruptive, these sardonic interjections break the rhythm of the chapter only to the degree that they usurp space within a temporally continuous context. Though most of the chapter is given over to dialogue, the narrator's voice is marked and consistent whether the passage relates to Bloom or Stephen. The stream of consciousness, on the other hand, after a by now typical opening segment, is muted in the second half of the chapter, where Stephen takes part in the conversation. For technical as well as strategic reasons, no attempt is made to juxtapose Stephen's and Bloom's thoughtstreams here or anywhere else in the novel. Interestingly, at the crucial second encounter with Crawford, Bloom's thoughts suddenly return to the page, registering his reaction not only to the rebuff but also to Stephen (147). On the other hand, at an equally crucial moment for Stephen, the spinning of the bitterly ironic

"Parable of the Plums," we have no record of his thought, or rather only the most sketchy and inconclusive record.

It is with some surprise and perhaps a bit of relief that we return in "Lestrygonians" to Bloom's stream of consciousness and the discreet and more than usually objective narrator. This use of an established convention is part of the alternate motion of the book's styles which frequently become more conservative before pushing on to new experiments. Effectively, "Lestrygonians" provides a buffer between "Aeolus" and "Scylla," which shocks us the more after the pause. (A similar tactic is noticeable in "Nausikaa," a placid contemplative interlude between two outrageous and hectic chapters.) The proliferating food and eating allusions that buttress the homeric analogy are not intrusive. Once again the monologue is broken by encounters, and, as in "Hades," the narrator wanders off to gather comments on Bloom, this time from disinterested and favorable parties.

"Aeolus" has prepared us for the more emphatic but subtler manipulations in "Scylla and Charybdis," where Joyce pits Stephen's increasingly lighthearted argument against his growing inner despair. In terms of the action, this contrast is pointed up when the sober and mystical AE exits shortly before an insouciant and ribald Mulligan enters to set a new tone. (Mulligan's farcical intrusion recalls Alcibiades' riotous entrance after Socrates' discourse in the *Symposium,* a parallel reinforced in Joyce's schema by a reference to Socrates and by the "technic" of this chapter: "dialectics.") The chapter is written in a medley of styles appropriate to the variety of functions it serves. At its center is the argument itself, rendered in the precise words of the participants, each of whom is characterized by a particular intellectual position and therefore by a particular rhetoric. Beyond this there is Stephen's playful but tense stream of consciousness loaded with freight for the argument, larded with ironic perceptions, increasingly private, but throughout, a fascinating performance. The narrator's relatively objective voice is complemented by a sharper, irreverent commentator reflecting on the action from Stephen's point of view. This puckish commentator contributes, not only the caricatural asides, but also the increasingly numerous typographical eccentricities: the dramatic dialogue that conveys Stephen's playful mood (203),[7] the second sequence in dialogue (209), which contains nothing to justify its format, and Mulligan's *dramatis personae* (216-17), which contrasts with and completes Best's playbill (187). Such devices suggest that the subject matter of the discussion is in itself dramatic and underscore the quality of Stephen's commitment to an argument he knows to be fruitless.

Up to "Wandering Rocks" the stream of consciousness has given us an approximation of two minds unraveling themselves in relation to a world full of opacities. Now the arranger begins to reduce these protagonists to the condition of the other characters, obliging us to reorient ourselves so that we may use our knowledge of Stephen and Bloom in contexts where their thought is jumbled, distorted, or absent. For the first and last time some of the minor characters come to us through their streams of consciousness (in Conmee's case mixed with indirect discourse). The strategy enables Joyce to present ironic foils for Stephen in little Dignam, who is also in mourning, for Bloom in the ineffectual commercial traveler Mr. Kernan, and for both together in Conmee, a figure who connects the two protagonists, being both a fatherly older man and religious in his orientation. This pivotal chapter is informed by cinematic montage which conveys a sense of simultaneity within a clearly delineated geographical space through a series of interlocking prose vignettes. The controlling images are church and state, Father Conmee and the viceregal procession. Their progress across town constitutes a narrative thread as fragile as their authority over the city and its concerns.[8] Throughout this chapter we are aware of being manipulated by the arranger, who insists on the spatial dimension by inserting incongruous reminders and breaking continuity to suggest the spontaneous rhythm of life seen in passing. Still, in sequence after sequence the narrator's voice gives us slight genre paintings, fragmentary in effect but complete in the manner of the epiphanies and firmly anchored in other aspects of the book. The chapter ends with a playful list of variously engaged spectators, enlivened by delightful and inappropriate details.

Beginning with the contrasting metallic notes of "Bronze by gold" and ending like the chapter with the patriotic "eppripfftaph" of Bloom's innocent anal salute, the overture of "Sirens" is a treasury of phrases torn from the chapter in order of their ap-

pearance. A fitting complement to the playful list of spectators at
the viceregal procession, it also sets the tone of this chaotic-seem-
ing chapter by giving musical or at least onomatopoetic form and
rhythmic diversity to prosaic circumstance. "Sirens" also pro-
longs the technique of "Wandering Rocks" by weaving the movements of Bloom, Boylan, and the blind stripling into the texture of
the bar scene. It goes far beyond "Scylla" in integrating (or orch-
estrating) event, occurring in different parts of the bar, interre-
lating through verbal *legerdemain* unrelated actions and producing
the effect of simultaneity. This is possible because, as in the following passage, the arranger irreverently but consistently distorts the
rhythm of the narrative voice:

> Bloowho went by by Moulang's pipes, bearing in his
> breast the sweets of sin, by Wine's antiques in memory
> bearing sweet sinful words, by Carroll's dusky battered
> plate, for Raoul.
> The boots to them, them in the bar, them barmaids
> came. For them unheeding him he banged on the counter
> his tray of chattering china. And (258)

Here the two dimensions (Bloom "bearing . . . the sweets of sin"
and the boots bearing a tray of tea), despite the misleading reference and the dislocations, are explicit enough, but the events
themselves are subjected to reduction and condensation. As a result of this technique, the reader is fully engaged by the verbal surface as an independent source of events and interest. While forcing
us to work harder and depriving us both of a firm narrative perspective and of Bloom's dependable voice, Joyce is working more
than ever against himself. His dislocations are possible and effective, however, because we have accumulated an awareness of
Bloom's mind and the Dublin scene. It is fitting that, when
Bloom's concerns come back into focus, even his thoughts are rendered comically random, captured, so to speak, by the sirens'
music to which he responds by picking up themes or falling into a
mental lilt.

Perhaps the most startling thing Joyce could do after the verbal
extravagance of "Sirens" was to reverse himself, returning not
only to the narrative tradition but apparently to oral narrative on a

very low popular level. "Cyclops" is sheer outrage and fun in all of its details, from the unidentified narrator, a cyclopean drink-cadging dun out of the middle depths of Dublin, to the balloon-popping interludes burlesquing a variety of subliterary genres. These asides are not part of the action, yet they grow naturally out of the context on which they comment so directly and expansively. Though they break the narrative rhythm, they do not distort the circumstance which reduces Bloom to an opacity if not a cliché, the scorned outsider whose increasing discomfort in the face of innuendo can only be surmised since we do not hear his thoughts. His behavior comes to us glossed by a character who knows how to spice a tale with malice:

> And Bloom, of course, with his knockmedown cigar putting on swank with his lardy face. Phenomenon! The fat heap he married is a nice old phenomenon with a back on her like a ballalley. (305)

This is the voice of Dublin giving us, for all its hyperbolic language, the "straight dope," a voice appropriate to low comedy, a genial mocker. It is also the voice of HCE's opponent in *Finnegans Wake,* Hosty, the down-and-outer who composes a scurrilous song to expose him to public scorn. The pace of the action itself is slow, the developmental rational, but the chapter reads, thanks to the comic trappings, like a farcical expansion of the muddled thought of the citizen and his drunken cronies. It contains Joyce's bitterest and broadest satire.

After the double-decked mockery of "Cyclops," the gentle mock-pastoral of "Nausikaa" seems tame, a rest for Bloom and the reader. It contains only one major innovation, an artificial voice in indirect inner discourse. Accustomed to receiving the unmediated thoughtstream, we are surprised and amused by this further breach of faith, but we have entered a stereotyped world and the sugary rhetoric is in keeping with the preciosity of the matter. Like the nude nymph on the Blooms' bedroom wall, Gerty is a figment of the male imagination even in her own eyes: a product, that is, of her wish to charm and of the religious training that has left her emotionally deprived. To emphasize this, Joyce interlards her monologue with snatches from the mass and permits Bloom to react in his own somewhat sweetened voice only after she has left. In order to join stylistically the opposite visions of Bloom and Gerty, Joyce narrates the whole chapter in a fittingly overripe prose. The "technic" is "tumescence detumescence," but with characteristic irony the swelling male role is given to a virgin and Bloom is left with the post-masturbatory mess. The deflated prose follows the curve of his fatigue.

"Nausikaa" mimes the perversion of sensibility. "Oxen of the Sun" deals, through its elaborate spoof on the history of English prose styles,* with the perversion of the intellect and the denial of nature. The tension between the rigidly stylized prose pastiches and the loose impiety and irreverence of the youths brings the reader further into the frame as an accomplice of the arranger, whose artificial disruption of the surface calls attenton to his ingenuity. More important, the verbal texture, which impedes rather than facilitates our attempts to follow the action it adorns, hacks away at the very possibility of communication while conveying the simple circumstance through a variety of absurdly dated and variously appropriate literary postures. This strategy brings writers from the past back to life to comment on a present which

---

* The limits of a particular style are worth noting, and we may be engaged by Joyce's working out the problem of adjusting his styles to fit or contrast with the event and by the verve of his imitation. It should be noted that, just as there are arranger-intrusions in the narrator-controlled daylight chapters and *vice versa,* there are snatches of the later styles in the early passages. Stuart Gilbert explains this in terms of the irregular development of the embryo. The following rough list should help the reader find his bearings.

Medieval Latin (383), Anglo-Saxon (384), Mandeville (386), Malory (387), Authorized Version and Browne (392), Bunyan (394), Pepys-Evelyn (396). Defoe (398), Swift (399), Addison (401), Sterne (404), Goldsmith (406), Burke (407), Junius (409), Gibbon (410), Radcliffe (412), Lamb (412), de Quincey (414), Landor (414), Macauley (416), Huxley (418), Dickens (420), Newman (421), Pater (422), Carlyle (423).

For further comment, see Gilbert (*James Joyce's "Ulysses": A Study*) [New York: Knopf, 1952], pp. 294–312, and James Atherton's "Oxen of the Sun" in Clive Hart and David Hayman, eds., *James Joyce's "Ulysses": Critical Essays* (Berkeley: University of California Press, 1974), as well as A. M. Klein's extremely elaborate analysis of the obstetrical metaphor in "Oxen of the Sun" (*Here and Now* 1 [January 1949]: 28–48).

casts their utterance in a fresh and generally comic light. However, the relationship of style to subject matter is not uniform. We may well question, for example, what is being deflated during the dickensian and carlylean commentaries on the Purefoys or how seriously we are to take Malory's Bloomish knight and Bunyan's characterization of Stephen as Boasthard. On the other hand, if many of the styles are inappropriately grave, some passages, especially those from the eighteenth century, like the unforgettable swiftian tale of the bull, are completely in keeping with the spirit of the moment.

In a more general sense, designed to suggest the stages in the development of the embryo, the "technic" provides a useful bridge between the two timeless circumstances: the fecund but sterile wit of the roistering bucks and the pathetic parturition that brings yet another Purefoy into Catholic Ireland. Everything conspires to distract us from the characters' dilemmas, effectively limiting their viability as individuals. Though both Bloom and Stephen are present and Stephen contributes actively to the conversation before his place is usurped by the better clown Mulligan, it is only to Bloom's thoughts that we are attuned, and these come to us mostly through a curtain of nineteenth-century styles. In "Circe," inner ferment will be conveyed as uproarious action; here, the din in the room is spoken about but not conveyed. Rather, the young men's exuberance and malice is stored up like the repressed concerns of Stephen and Bloom or like the tardy infant until, in the concluding passage, we burst the sack and the prose breaks out of its formal limits to become the direct if fragmentary expression of animal spirits. It is in these last pages, punctuated by the apocalyptic jargon of the American, Dowie, that most of the action occurs. But, if the earlier styles are often opaque, this literally transcribed but fragmentary utterance deprived of all narrational controls pulls us up short. What has occurred, if not precisely a riot, is an intellectual chaos appropriate to the drunken high spirits that bear psychic fruit in the next chapter.

"Circe," which places Bloom and Stephen as reactors to subconscious impulses in the center of an imaginary stage, combines techniques and effects from its literary models (*Faust* and *The Temptation of Saint Anthony*) with others from the traditional pantomime.

Bloom and Stephen, after having been flattened out in the previous chapters are here emotionally inverted. The stage directions enable Joyce to project the contents of their minds on a screen of opaque and pedestrian activity. Even more striking is our sense that we are part of this scene, as baffled by the nightlight as they are, as bewitched. The nighttown context, for all of this, is kept clear enough so that we can divine, if we keep our eyes open, approximately where illusion meets fact. On the other hand, though the major hallucinatory sequences are carefully set off from each other and the chapter is artfully subdivided into dramatic acts and scenes, the arranger makes no clear distinction between minor hallucinations and the normal surface and even introduces improbable elements into the characters' hallucinations. As a result, the visions and identities of Stephen and Bloom are blurred, universalized, mythicized; the components of their days are intermingled, so that their fates may momentarily be joined. Since the technique makes no formal distinction between the levels of experience, this is technically easy enough to accomplish. But the amount of fact, theme, and analogy juggling it required was staggering. Joyce seems to have taken the whole book, jumbled it together in a giant mixer and then rearranged its elements in a monster pantomime which, as is proper, includes every imaginable form of foolery but which may well be the most serious chapter in the book, a true rite of passage.

In "Eumaeus" we relapse from chaos to platitude in a tired, threadbare, flatulent narrative larded with the sort of commonplaces that would fill the mouth of Sancho Panza and please Flaubert. At University College Joyce delighted in the chronicle of Bouvard and Pécuchet, those two bumbling penpushers for whom Flaubert wrote his *Dictionary of Commonplaces*.[9] Here Joyce seems to be cramming all that the French writer knew on the subject into one short chapter which uses style to conceal sensibility but tickle the sense of humor. Like Flaubert, he ironically vindicates the norm (as opposed to the establishment) by demonstrating its capacity to generate a pathos that is beyond its comprehension. It is the voice and not the point of view that is Bloom's, and it is through the voice that the arranger conveys with surprising accuracy the drink- and fatigue-dulled sentiments of both protagonists. There is no stream of consciousness and only a hint of the early narrator, and despite the occasional nod toward Stephen, the chapter is dominated by Bloom's reflections on just about everything. The technique is parody only in the loosest sense, parody of a Bloomish mind turned inside out in a way that contrasts with the "Circe" inversion. It is a mind with its defenses up and not down, one which has turned suddenly public in the manner of a conventional and self-deceiving narrator. The result is ridiculous in a way that the stream of consciousness never is, but the point is not only that Bloom, like his style, is tired, but that the tired voice tries to convince us it has something to say.

In "Ithaca," the arranger, who has teased us through "Eumaeus," dons the mask of perverse objectivity. Like the "narrative (old)," the "catechism (impersonal)" seems precisely wrong for conveying a human situation and rewarding the reader who has warmed to the characters' predicament. Yet, in both chapters, the style permits Joyce to convey the inevitable resolution of an impossible relationship without resorting to brutal irony or maudlin sentiment. The questions and responses range from the most objective to the most personal, the language from the least to the most expressive. Increasingly, graphic passages function as seriocomic intrusions on the grave proceedings. In a sense this chapter, which, as though in an afterthought, carries so much of the book's exposition, is the warmest of them all. This is largely because, despite his elaborate pose, the speaker is not completely reliable and his point of view is not always clear. He is after all a projection of Bloom's scientific mentality rather than of the spirit of inquiry pure and simple. For the first and only time we see Bloom and Stephen in conjunction as reactors, and we can measure the humanity of each on a minimal level which puts similarities and differences in sharp, humorous, and human relief. The technique is especially efficient at boiling down thought to the level of reflex, and in this sense both protagonists are comically stripped of their intellectual masks and rendered both vulnerable and human on a level at which Molly, however slight her motherly instinct, can approach and identify them.

After apparently draining his personae of all life, rendering them equal to the stars as constellated facts, distant and flickering,

Joyce suddenly returns us to the earth in "Penelope." To accomplish this he concocted a medium designed to carry everything like the river Liffey in *Finnegans Wake,* which carries civilized humanity out to the sea for replenishment. Molly's monologue is an extreme form of stream of consciousness, so extreme that it brings us close to the conventions of the dramatic soliloquy in which the character must locate himself and describe his own behavior. Molly reacts to virtually nothing but herself reacting to recollected experience on a sensual level. Deprived of external controls, her monologue is apparently formless. Details and motives tend to flow together and personages to blend in ways that they cannot flow or blend anywhere else. Yet we can trace the development of Molly's thought, and we will automatically supply the missing punctuation so that Joyce has it both ways. Further, there are eight sentences which can be regarded as units of action. The openness of the form is comparable to the openness of "Circe" where themes and natures meet, identities are dissolved and blended. Here, on the other hand, character, the naturalistic sheath, is fixed, resolved, and related. The flowing prose of Molly reconstitutes, on a level that is less abstract than it has yet been, a reality mauled by the evening chapters. In the middle of the night we see things clearly for the first time, as though from the other side of experience, by the light of the moon.

Textural Considerations

The larger stylistic and technical shifts which mark the chapters of *Ulysses* are bound to attract more attention as symptoms of Joyce's virtuosity and to demand more justification as functional aspects of the book. But a study of style and technique must not neglect the smaller units, the sentences, paragraphs, and passages on which Joyce lavished such attention and which carry the main weight of his innovations and conceal, or rather reveal through suggestion, so many of the book's delights, far more in fact than any critic can disclose. An examination of almost any of these lesser segments is rather like a visit to the famous mausoleum of Galla Placidia in Ravenna, one of the gems of Italian Byzantine art. Entering a round chamber lit only by slits of windows paned with thin sheets of alabaster, we gaze about us at the vague mosaics that completely cover the inner walls and dome. Gradually, as our eyes accustom themselves to the light, details begin to appear, first the grosser and then the subtler, asserting themselves until they fill our sight beyond our capacity to apprehend them with a procession of sparkling images. If we allow for the difference in medium and the greater complexity of Joyce's vision, *Ulysses* is like a series of such chambers through which we pass rapidly, carrying with us images of all sorts in vital interaction and subject individually to further elaboration, images which, even half-seen, help compose our vision and create an impression of an organic whole. Though a comprehensive unraveling of the book would be impossible and probably counterproductive, it is well to look closely once in a while if only to appreciate the effects we have been subjected to and to apply that understanding to an appreciation of the book's subject matter. In this we return, as we must, to a unitary view of manner and matter and a sense of Joyce's total accomplishment.

Some of the densest passages fall in the earlier, more conventional chapters. Note in the following passage from ''Telemachus'' the alliterative effects, the deliberately repeated words and phrases (a common device in the *Portrait*), the curious perspectives and ambiguities designed to enforce juxtapositions, the shifts in mood and tone, and the synesthesia in May Dedalus' ''mute, reproachful'' ''breath'':

> —But a lovely mummer, he murmured to himself. Kinch, the loveliest mummer of them all.
>
> He shaved evenly and with care, in silence, seriously.
>
> Stephen, an elbow rested on the jagged granite, leaned his palm against his brow and gazed at the fraying edge of his shiny black coat-sleeve. Pain, that was not yet the pain of love, fretted his heart. Silently, in a dream she had come to him after her death, her wasted body within its loose brown graveclothes giving off an odour of wax and rosewood, her breath, that had bent upon him, mute, reproachful, a faint odour of wetted ashes. Across the threadbare cuffedge he saw the sea hailed as a great sweet mother by

the wellfed voice beside him. The ring of bay and skyline held a dull green mass of liquid. A bowl of white china had stood beside her deathbed holding the green sluggish bile which she had torn up from her rotting liver by fits of loud groaning vomiting. (5)

This passage, simple enough for Joyce, is not free of elliptical phrases or ambiguous reference. What is the source of the "pain, that was not yet the pain of love"? Is it a sense of physical bereavement, or is it a reflection on friendship and betrayal, or again is it Stephen's own sense of the void of affection, his inability to achieve the distance from himself that would enable him to love another? Within a neat tripartite paragraph, we find a poignant opposition between the sunny scene and the morbid memory, between Stephen's self-concern reflected in the "threadbare cuff-edge" and Mulligan's "wellfed voice." Playing against our expectations, Joyce gives us the "cuffedge" rather than the bay as the object of Stephen's gaze.

Skirting the thin edge of bathos or rather pushing beyond bathos, he counters the dream image ("in a dream she had come") with the gross details of the death throes, all the more moving because they are sparked by Mulligan's facile Swinburnean image of the sea as a "great sweet mother" (5). The carefully elaborated equation of the sea first to a bowl of vomit and then death gives us in slow motion a foretaste of Stephen's stream of consciousness. The process is also mythologizing, for, by virtue of the highly charged language, the concatenation sea-mother-death-guilt-revulsion becomes at once unstable and indissoluble. From another point of view, the reader participates in a secondary creative process, being privy both to the banal stimuli and to the elaboration of an exceptional reaction which is not too far below the level of esthetic production. Joyce is forever emphasizing Stephen's role as the latent artist. At this point, however, as opposed to "Proteus," he is careful to give the words to the narrator, who weaves Stephen's impressions and characterizes for us a mind we have yet to inspect.

This is the first statement of the ghost-dream motive which partly motivates Stephen's distress and justifies his search for a mother substitute in the style of Ann Hathaway. The dream resolves itself finally in its hallucinated antistatement of "Circe" where it finds its comic-pathetic counterpart in Bloom's vision of Rudy. But in this book of waking visions, the ghost-dream does not stand alone. Haines has dreamt of the "black panther," an identity later bestowed on Bloom. Bloom has dreamt of Molly in Eastern garb, a dream fulfilled imaginatively in "Circe" and realistically when Molly plans to buy herself such an outfit in "Penelope." Stephen has dreamt of meeting a man who offers him a melon and promises unknown pleasures, and this dream is fulfilled by his meeting with Bloom who offers him a liaison with Molly and who comically completes the action by his final "melonsmellonous osculation" (735). Stephen's dreams are respectively western (or of death and the night in relation to the sun's motion) and eastern (or of life and promise as reflected in Bloom's musings on the eastward journey in "Calypso")[10] (60–61).

By page 6 of *Ulysses,* the narrator who has spoken for Stephen and engaged us in his experience begins to recede, allowing Stephen to speak for himself. In the following passage their voices almost imperceptibly mingle:

> Stephen bent forward and peered at the mirror held out to him, cleft by a crooked crack, hair on end. As he and others see me. Who chose this face for me? This dogsbody to rid of vermin. It asks me too. (6)

Even before Stephen begins to speak to himself, the associative line has been established. He looks *at* the mirror before he looks in. He sees the crack with which he instinctively associates his own appearance and by extension his condition so that the two images blend and clash confusedly as would a single image viewed in a cracked glass. In accord with the image, the shift from objective to subjective utterance is abrupt but not jarring. Stephen seems to be objective only about his own reflection. Later, we can contrast this "objectivity" with that of Bloom seeing himself through the eyes of his cat or in a variety of reflecting surfaces. Like the key, whose abandonment is one of the major symbolic actions of this chapter, and like the dreams, the mirror becomes a multivalent motif.

The question of identity and the related problem of parenthood are introduced when Stephen asks, "Who chose this face for me?" For Stephen, the face reflected in a mirror is but a shadow that can mask an identity, just as the body can provide the soul with a temporary case. Accordingly, physical relationships are unstable, and Stephen's father, "man with my voice and my eyes" (38), and his sister Dilly ("My eyes they say she has . . . Shadow of my mind" [243].) should have no claims on him. As his reactions repeatedly show, however, he is unable to sever himself, to reject, in the manner of that fiery Irish saint Columbanus, or of Christ, the enforced relationship without severe conscience qualms, or "agenbite of inwit." His mask of strength is a mask for weakness. He holds too hard to the here and now to risk the necessary loss of an identity which is as yet insufficiently established. Thus we are brought back to the image in the split mirror, in which confused life is captured.

Stephen's problem is then not one of simple acceptance or rejection but of how to accept and reject simultaneously, how to be of and above the world, how to be a creator, that is, one who projects out of his substance a new life which he does not live, an action which implies the acceptance of that substance in the first place. Thus he must face not only the reflection in the mirror but the image reflected, his "hair on end," his face, his "dogsbody to rid of vermin." The latter, a corollary to the vision of putrefaction in the dream passage examined earlier, underlines the nature of filth and vermin or of mortal misery which he strives at great expense to surmount by the spirit. It is appropriate that in "Circe," in the midst of vital corruption, Stephen first comes to grips with his identity and into contact with the flesh (to say nothing of the fist) of others. Meanwhile, we have no description here of Stephen, but only a synecdoche: his hair in disarray, a condition most of us share when we get up from the bed but from which Mulligan's uncombed hair is exempt. For the rest, in stark contrast to the detailed and suggestive portrait of Mulligan, we have a sense of Stephen as disembodied, clothed in the cast-offs of an unknown or, worse, in the boots of a Buck, treating his flesh as a confession box for the spirit.

In "Proteus," after experimenting with the "ineluctable modality of the audible," Stephen opens his eyes to see a bitter travesty of birth amidst desolation in the Irish wasteland. His response is a flood of imagery richer even than the reality apprehended by Bloom but deriving from his hoard of knowledge-nuts imaginatively reconstituted:

> They came down the steps from Leahy's terrace prudently, *Frauenzimmer:* and down the shelving shore flabbily their splayed feet sinking in the silted sand. Like me, like Algy, coming down to our mighty mother. Number one swung lourdily her midwife's bag, the other's gamp poked in the beach. From the liberties, out for the day. Mrs Florence MacCabe, relict of the late Patk MacCabe, deeply lamented, of Bride Street. One of her sisterhood lugged me squealing into life. Creation from nothing. What has she in the bag? A misbirth with a trailing navelcord, hushed in ruddy wool. The cords of all link back, strandentwining cable of all flesh. That is why mystic monks. Will you be as gods? Gaze in your omphalos. Hello. Kinch here. Put me on to Edenville. Aleph, alpha: nought, nought, one. (37–38)

While the playful narrator imposes poetic effects on prosy circumstance, Stephen speaks a sort of poetry in hard nuggets of prose. The contrast is deliberate and effective. We are aware that the first and third sentences record Stephen's impressions, while the rest deal with his reactions. The weak rhymes ("prudently" and "flabbily" echoed and reenforced by the contrived "lourdily"), the alliteration verging on onomatopoeia which follows a deliberately undistinguished opening, and the ambiguous reference in "flabbily" capture the movement and the appearance of the two sleazy females. To suggest sterility and closed options, the narrator joins with a comma two absurdly complementary ideas. One "midwife," playing the feminine role with masculine vigor, carries the heavy bag, an insufficient womb, complete with inadequate babe. The other carries the male implement, an umbrella, which she pokes into the barren sand. The image is all the more effective in the light of its analogue from the "Parable of the Plums," in which these same "Dublin vestals" project plum pits from the top of the Nelson pillar in another mock-fertility rite.

Significantly, Stephen's first reaction is to begin composing the parable, starting as he does in "Aeolus" and later in "Scylla" with "local colour" (188). This should be followed, in accordance with his good Jesuit training, by "composition of place," but instead it leads him into a meditation on origins. Quickly abandoning his composition, Stephen asks "What has she in the bag?" Then, in the spirit of his dogsbody reference in "Telemachus," he identifies with the "misbirth,"[11] which he brings into misbegotten life and imaginatively returns to the womb for an umbilical telephone conversation with the primal mother who, as we soon learn, should have no navel. Further, through the mystic telephone number ("Aleph, alpha: nought, nought, one"), he suggests that he too is a terminus, the omega or zero to Adam's alpha or one, thus predicting the apocalypse and casting himself in the role of Christ. Here too is the theosophical response to the problem of history and identity and Stephen's mockery of it, mockery that is not devoid of disappointment at another failed solution. The question Stephen wishes to ask of the lady in Edenville (both Eden and Edenborough) is perhaps the same he tries to ask his mother in "Circe." Through the medium of this paragraph, despite the jangle of moods, modes, voices, and attitudes, Joyce effectively takes us from a simple realistic statement to the breakdown of communication into letters, numbers, and mystic symbols for the ineffable which Stephen so bitterly mocks.

Stephen is much less his own man than he would like to be. Not only does he lean on his training (turning it of course to new ends), but also, as the interpolated second sentence shows, he returns automatically even in the privacy of his thoughts to Mulligan, whose words and behavior dominate his day almost as much as Molly's words and behavior dominate Bloom's, but to opposite effect. Stephen's play with Mulligan's Swinburne is especially significant in view of Buck's attempt to relate his Jesuit training to his failure as a poet: "They drove his wits astray . . . by visions of hell," Buck tells Haines in "Wandering Rocks." "He will never capture the Attic note. The note of Swinburne, of all poets, the white death and the ruddy birth. That is his tragedy. He can never be a poet" (249).[12] Here, in this most solipsistic of passages which speaks of urgent concerns, Buck speaks through the image of the "misbirth . . . hushed in ruddy wool," through the nickname Kinch, through the omphalos reference, and probably even through the playful device of the spirit telephone call.

Given the quality of his mind and predilections, we may expect Bloom's mental stream to be far less dense in ideas and allusions than Stephen's. Still, we find in a characteristic passage a remarkable density and luminosity of effects and similar though perhaps less startling juxtapositions. Take, for example, this bit from Bloom's frustrating conversation with M'Coy in "Lotus Eaters":

> —I was with Bob Doran, he's on one of his periodical bends, and what do you call him Bantam Lyons. Just down there in Conway's we were.
>
> Doran, Lyons in Conway's. She raised a gloved hand to her hair. In came Hoppy. Having a wet. Drawing back his head and gazing far from beneath his veiled eyelids he saw the bright fawn skin shine in the glare, the braided drums. Clearly I can see today. Moisture about gives long sight perhaps. Talking of one thing or another. Lady's hand. Which side will she get up? (74)

Three actions are made simultaneous in this passage: the narration of the meeting with Hoppy Holohan (a Dublin character who plays a minor but amusing part in the story "A Mother"), M'Coy's conversation through which the tale impinges on Bloom's consciousness, and the gently erotic vision of the "haughty" lady adjusting her gloves across the street. Add to this Bloom's sense of himself and his modest experiment with the light ("Clearly I can see today."). It is in the spirit of this chapter that the levels, though disparate, do not clash dramatically. We may however smile at the juxtaposition of Bloom's lust and his scientific interest while he is listening to the small talk of a cadger angling for the loan of a piece of luggage. As usual, the subtler verbal effects are in the narrator's voice. Bloom's reflections on the lady are no match for what we know he sees. Paradoxically, what he sees is erotic only in its expression which must correspond to his apprehension. Joyce is doing in his second sentence precisely the sort of thing he has done in the *Portrait* (see the bird-girl of chapter 4), where a minimal gesture is invested with erotic power. The prospect of the "bright fawn skin" suggests brighter prospects, while the military and masterful tone of "braided drums" goes beyond the object described, giving an early instance of Bloom's masochism. The gesture, whose grace we must imagine, fills us, like Bloom, with mute anticipation. Playing with Bloom, teasing us, withholding the proffered rewards, however slight they may be, the narrator is at his best when, a few lines after our paragraph, he mentions, "High brown boots with laces dangling," and then has Bloom reflect, "Proud: rich: silk stockings." Saying nothing, exposing nothing, he has suggested an object worthy of our expectant gaze and prepared us humorously to be comically let down by the carefully isolated couplet which culminates the passage:

> Watch! Watch! Silk flash rich stockings white. Watch!
> A heavy tramcar honking its going slewed between. (74)

Every item in our paragraph will reappear elsewhere, as will the emotional climate. The sensual moment is fulfilled in "Nausikaa" and travestied in "Circe." The conversation with M'Coy is increased a thousandfold in "Cyclops," where the incident he recites is given an amusing twist by Bob Doran, deeper than ever in his cups, who explodes into incredulous surprise on hearing the news, for the second time (302–303). Bloom's experiment foreshadows his self-exploration in the second half of "Nausikaa." His thirsty but innocent gaze is more than matched by Stephen's guilty mocking memory in "Proteus": "You prayed to the devil in Serpentine avenue that the fubsy widow in front might lift her clothes still more from the wet street" (40). Ultimately each of these and other echoes must be taken into consideration as qualities latent in this passage.

Bloom's stream of consciousness is always readily identifiable. Despite the arranger's manipulation of his thought and the shifts in tone and emphasis, it retains throughout a vigor at once naïve and inventive that reflects on his native intelligence and maintains our respect even in his darkest hour. In the following paragraph of unmediated thought, Bloom, who has just left the Ormand bar in "Sirens," is walking to the music of a band:

> Instruments. A blade of grass, shell of her hands, then blow. Even comb and tissuepaper you can knock a tune out

of. Molly in her shift in Lombard street west, hair down. I
suppose each kind of trade made its own, don't you see?
Hunter with a horn. Haw. Have you the? *Cloche. Sonnez la!*
Shepherd his pipe. Policeman a whistle. Locks and keys!
Sweep! Four o'clock's all's well! Sleep! All is lost now.
Drum? Pompedy. Wait, I know. Towncrier, bumbailiff.
Long John. Waken the dead. Pom. Dignam. Poor little
nominedomine. Pom. It is music, I mean of course it's all
pom pom pom very much what they call *da capo.* Still you
can hear. As we march we march along, march along.
Pom. (289)

Here the musical references provide most of the substance and
even dictate the tempo, but the randomness, the spirit of inquiry,
the rhetorical level is unmistakably Bloomish. It is past four and
Boylan has reached Molly, the ultimate siren in this chapter full of
mantraps. Ulysses-Bloom, drawn to her but paralysed by fear and
guilt, resists her charms when he decides through indecision not to
follow Boylan. Joyce insists on Molly's siren nature in the first part
of the paragraph when he has Bloom view her hand as a shell and
associate the comb with her long hair. In the previous paragraph,
Bloom and the blind stripling (Stephen's surrogate) have sailed
past the portrait of a cigarette-ad siren with her "hair all stream-
ing," and earlier the barmaids behind their reef of counter have
listened to a shell. But the allusion is important mainly as a symptom of Bloom's mental anguish as repeatedly he tries to turn his
thoughts away from 7 Eccles Street and repeatedly he fails. The
appropriateness of the musical comb to woman combined with the
vision of Molly in her shift during happier times lead him to begin
working out the origins of musical instruments, or rather to begin
a forced inner conversation complete with a nervous "don't you
see." Unfortunately, the hunter's horn, his first example of an instrument made by members of a trade, has sexual implications and
worse. Hunter is the name of a watch which reminds him of the
time of Boylan's appointment and, by virtue of his misunderstand-
ing of the French *"cloche"* (bell), of the erotic play which helped
Boylan prepare himself to pursue his quarry. Bloom quickly shifts
to the shepherd's pipe which brings to mind the policeman and by
extension the fact that he is at this moment being robbed. Locks

and keys refer not only to protection but also to the lack of protection.[13] Not only is Bloom keyless, but, as we read in "Nausikaa," "Love laughs at locksmiths" (364); given the nature of his marriage, his key would offer slight protection. Perhaps thinking of another way to enter a house, he turns again to his obsession, for the sweep (whose only instrument is a phallic broom) calls to mind the rhyme "sleep" and once more the time of Boylan's appointment, disguised as a towncrier's "Four o'clock's all's well!" Apparently, there is no escape through logic, and in fact "All is lost now."[14] So he turns quickly and in desperation to the sounds around him, the sounds of the band that pulls him into marching step, dragging his thoughts into its catchy rhythmical nothought, free at last.

In this paragraph as in many others the thought serves as a screen through which meanings are perceived. At the same time it helps convey the man in the fullness of his experience with poignant immediacy and illustrates one of the functions of his feverish associations, namely, to mask his anxiety, guilt feelings, and insecurity not from the world but from himself. It is worth noting how well stocked his mind is with objects and objective associations and how cleverly he can relate those items which are not derived from automatic associations. It is also characteristic of him that his thought is too weak to resist intrusions, but strong enough to carry him through a number of barriers. Thus he does not abandon the thread of trades until the emotional pressure and the insistent rhythm render thought impossible.

The kaleidoscopic treatment of events in "Circe" may be seen as one sort of extension for the multiplication of objects and obsessions in Bloom's stream of consciousness. Another sort is available in the following excerpt from "Eumaeus" in which Bloom's immediate subject is the talkative sailor, whose lies give this chapter its homeric flavor:

> However, reverting to friend Sinbad and his horrifying adventures (who reminded him a bit of Ludwig, *alias* Ledwidge, when he occupied the boards of the Gaiety when Michael Gunn was identified with the management in the *Flying Dutchman*, a stupendous success, and his host of admirers came in large numbers, everyone simply flocking to

hear him though ships of any sort, phantom or the reverse,
on the stage usually fell a bit flat as also did trains), there
was nothing intrinsically incompatible about it, he con-
ceded. On the contrary, that stab in the back touch was
quite in keeping with those Italianos, though candidly he
was none the less free to admit those ice creamers and friers
in the fish way, not to mention the chip potato variety and
so forth, over in little Italy there, near the Coombe, were
sober thrifty hardworking fellows except perhaps a bit too
given to pothunting the harmless necessary animal of the
feline persuasion . . . (636–37)

Held by our expectation that something significant will take place
when the two wanderers are joined, rewarded by the scraps of action that filter through, we are teased and diverted by a rhetoric
which might belong to the Bloomish author of a prize titbit. As
some of Samuel Beckett's voices have shown us, there is esthetic
and metaphysical merit in saying so little and suggesting so much.
We hang on through the irrelevant parentheses, the journalistic
circumlocutions, the needless qualifications, the nonsequitors, the
mixed metaphors, the senseless affectations, the malapropisms, the
redundancies, indeed through a catalog of rhetorical sins that
vies for completeness with the battery of rhetorical devices used
in "Aeolus" to support the windy metaphor. All the while we
know that Bloom, who has no real point to make, is fooling himself
more than Stephen, who could not care less. Our most immediate
rewards are the verbal accidents (as numerous as the objects and
events that animate Bloom's monologues) which have usurped the
role of action and experience and which absorb us as would some
fantastic conjuring trick. Will the narrator be able to find a new
obstacle to expression, a new source of embarrassment to flaunt
our need to sustain Bloom in the presence of his young judge? Just
when we know he must have finished, we find that he has another
rabbit, and another. In our comic desperation we grab for the first
solid fact that comes our way, even the hilarious description of the
only Italians Bloom has seen, "those ice creamers and friers in the
fish way, not to mention the chip potato variety and so forth, over
in little Italy there, near the Coombe." Reading such a passage is

like grasping a bubble or a spirit, or the essence of the divine, but then we may wonder what God the Father had to say to his only son in paradise. Having subsumed everything through his experience, Bloom, like God, knows nothing.

The narrative strategy here makes us accomplices in unveiling the one who reveals. At the same time it mutes and mimes the drama of the encounter. Paradoxically, we are being served up Bloom's stream of consciousness grotesquely distorted and diluted as narrative or rather as a narrative account of a conversation. We are as usual aware of the sources of Bloom's ideas, and we may also sense that the same process that led to Stephen's brilliant compositions here leads to dull-thudding and hilarious banality. Still, though the narrator is probably accurate about the content, Bloom could never be this humorless and pedestrian in his expression. The least sympathetic of his commentators is kinder to him than this literary projection. Faced with an unfriendly witness like the narrator of "Cyclops," we are willing to discount even the truth and sympathize with a well-meaning bumbler in a tight spot. Faced with a friendly but inept one, we are forced to laugh twice through our sympathy and admit even in the absence of other evidence that the little dun is right: "if you said to Bloom: *Look at, Bloom. Do you see that straw? That's a straw.* Declare to my aunt he'd talk about it for an hour so he would and talk steady" (316).

Like Ulysses at the swineherd's, the usually forthright traveler can be astonishingly devious, but unlike his model, he is a poor dissembler. It is not so much his transparent motives as what he unconsciously says that enthralls us. The references to such travelers as Sinbad and the Flying Dutchman recall the Wandering Jew and Ulysses and the unquiet ghosts that haunt both men. The *"alias"* which does not conceal suggests the disguises of Ulysses but conveys the inadequate masks of Bloom himself and underlines his pathetic ineptness at this moment. The pantomime at the Gaiety continues a motif introduced through Stephen's musings in "Telemachus" (10). Here it adds the dimension of sentimental farce and points back to "Circe." When Bloom mentions that Ludwig's "host of admirers came in large numbers," we may recall his slip in "Cyclops" ("the wife's admirers" [313]) and discover another even more Freudian slip in the play on ejaculation. The remainder of the paragraph contains a slur on the Italians which, though gentle and, like all of Bloom's expressions of sentiment, well-meant, echoes anti-Semitic clichés. Bloom's real point, concealed by an inept subterfuge, is that passion is exciting and his Mediterranean Molly is passionate; his real need is to share her with Stephen, to make himself interesting through her glamour, to air his obsession, and to express obliquely his distress over her adultery. Ironically, he is exposing himself as a naïve and home-loving romantic to the guilty romantic who has earlier glamourized the wanderer in the Jew.

It is tempting to round out this discussion of Joyce's effects as they relate to meaning by treating briefly his handling of one of the book's minor cruxes, the infidelity of Molly as attested to by the list of twenty-five lovers (not suitors) in "Ithaca." For all its apparent objectivity, the list, like other items in this chapter, is a delightful fraud or at least an equivocation. We read: "Assuming Mulvey to be the first term of his series, Penrose, Bartell d'Arcy, professor Goodwin, Julius Mastiansky, John Henry Menton, Father Bernard Corrigan . . . Hugh E. (Blazes) Boylan and so each and so on to nolast term" (731). Though most readers fail to notice, this is "his," that is, Bloom's account and hence of doubtful value if not simply a projection of his masochistic fancy. The narrator has done little more than arrange the "lovers" chronologically. No wonder some of the individual items are absurd and Lieutenant Gardner, one of Molly's most ardent suitors (749), is omitted. Still, we fall readily into the trap prepared for us by the arranger who, playing on our prior hearsay knowledge, permits us to turn the neophyte adulteress into a whore. In this way the naturalistic texture is both subverted and maintained and Molly's symbolic eminence established. The joke on us is a serious one, a function of the style and a reflection of a possible reality. Molly *could be* a great whore and the *Magna Mater*, but she *is* a lazy, ignorant bundle of instincts tied to middle class values, though endowed with a fairly good singing voice, a hot temper, a sense of humor, and ample dimensions. If the superobjective voice of "Ithaca" fails to tell us this, the subjective effusion of "Penelope" reveals all, giving the lie to the list and altering many of our preconceptions. One example will suffice to illustrate the efficacy of Joyce's methods:

> . . . I wish some man or other would take me sometime when hes there and kiss me in his arms theres nothing like a kiss long and hot down to your soul almost paralyses you then I hate that confession when I used to go to Father Corrigan he touched me father and what harm if he did where and I said on the canal bank like a fool but whereabouts on your person my child on the leg behind high up was it yes rather high up . . . I always think of the real father what did he want to know for when I already confessed it to God he had a nice fat hand the palm moist always I wouldn't [sic] mind feeling it neither would he Id say by the bullneck in his horsecollar . . . I could see his face he couldnt see mine of course hed never turn or let on still his eyes were red when his father died theyre lost for a woman of course must be terrible when a man cries let alone them Id like to be embraced by one in his vestments . . . (740–41)

We can scratch Father Corrigan from Bloom's list, or can we? Molly has enjoyed him in the abstract if not in the flesh, and the Bible speaks of ocular lust. If Molly's desire turns out to be not much stronger than Bloom's voyeuristic impulses, her expression of desire ("a kiss long and hot down to your soul almost paralyses you") has the validity of Stephen's imaginings in "Proteus" (49). To our minds there is only a superficial difference between these vivid fantasies and the actions they describe. It is worth noting that Molly's yearning is more appropriate to an adolescent than to a hardened woman. Still, she has had no relations with a priest, and she will go on to disprove most of the list in detail and to show herself to be even less worldly than Bloom and almost as faithful as Penelope.

    The most striking effect of Molly's utterance is the flow conveyed not only by the lack of punctuation but also by the tone and especially by the proliferation of pronouns. When, rather than complete the sentence beginning "when I used to go to Father Corrigan," Molly begins a new one with the ambiguous "he

touched me," she provides the hint followed up later with her reflections on his "fat hand." In a parallel development Bloom is
subtly identified with the priest through the title "father" which
reminds Molly "of the real father" and generates the aside, "still
[Poldy's] eyes were red when his father died." Molly's undirected
thought has led her to make a statement that reflects not only on
her husband's curious abstinence but also on her unconscious wish
that he resume relations. It is the reader, encouraged by the fluid
juxtaposition, who completes both the identification and the
thought. The closer we inspect this or any passage from Molly's
monologue the richer its implications become. We may point in
passing to the priestly hands, so important in the *Portrait* as em-
blems of another sort of humanity, or to the confession, which is
focal to Stephen's experience and foreign to Bloom's, or to the pa-
ternity theme, or to "paralysis," which characterizes the Dublin
scene as well as the lives of Molly and Bloom, or to the bulls and
horses seen among other things as sacrificial animals and fertility
symbols. Each of them is touched lightly here. Like her reputation,
Molly's monologue can carry or dissolve anything. It is the ideal
response both to male objectivity and to the crystalline profusion of
"Circe" since it naturalizes excess through verbal illusion. Recalling the sort of magic that joins Stephen to Buck in "Telemachus," we see that in this sense too Joyce has come full circle,
elaborating a style whose very simplicity and directness can prove
endlessly evocative.

Conclusion

If, as experience shows, even the most straightforward plot summary will contain errors, the critical study, because it defends a position, is bound to limit if not distort its object. It follows that no book on *Ulysses* will do justice to it. Still, we can learn from even the clumsiest effort, and this brief attempt to number the book's qualities may give the reader a sense of it as complex and coherent, austere and comic, difficult and accessible, capable of stirring us in many ways but always in terms of itself. If the reality we perceive there is a mirror of the everyday in terms of the singular, the singular thus perceived is increasingly familiar and dynamic and very like our own singularity. The object of our contemplation and our experience of it are increasingly one. But it is not in terms of the end result that we should think of this book but rather of the process of apprehension. Our movement through it is its own reward and is virtually endless, for the object will never be fully perceived. *Ulysses* can be seen as a collection of skillfully arranged vibrations whose intensity will depend on our awareness of them and whose number is variable. The source of these vibrations is the tension set up among the qualities which I have tried to describe (and others beyond the scope of so short a study). It follows that we cannot define *Ulysses* in terms of any one aspect though we may give precedence to its narrative and dramatic content. Further, in a work that uses the moment to suggest eternity and the geographical point to suggest infinity, there can be no more question of moral positions than there can be of conclusions.

Finally, there is the question of judgment. There are certainly flaws in the fabric of *Ulysses,* imbalance, overingenious symbolism, dead spaces filled by the author's wit, but the ultimate criteria in this case should be the book's vitality and the seemingly inexhaustible interest it generates in generations of readers. And besides, who can sort out flaws in the three-ring circus where in the turbulence of the endless moment each individual flaw resists detection or pales to insignificance? The negative criticism of *Ulysses* that most affected Joyce during his lifetime was in Wyndham Lewis' *Time and Western Man* which among other things attacked Joyce as a follower of Bergson and Einstein and labeled Bloom a stage Jew standing in for Joyce himself. Joyce responded obliquely, as was his wont, but at length in *Finnegans Wake*. To Frank Budgen he said, "Allowing that the whole of what Lewis says about my book is true, is it more than ten percent of the truth?"

Ten Years After Thoughts

Constraints of space, combined with the need to give a fresh global reading of an inexhaustible text, made it inevitable that just about every aspect of this guide to *Ulysses* could be greatly expanded. The novel is, after all, an open invitation to endless analysis, and the critic's job is to suggest directions in which that analysis can go rather than to exhaust the possibilities of any one method or tack. The reader and other critics should not be deprived, as Mallarmé said, of the "delicious joy of creating."

Through the years there has been ample evidence that *The Mechanics of Meaning* (a title thought up on the spur of the moment and without any structuralist, semiological, or reader-response proddings) has performed precisely the function of opening fresh paths for critics ranging from the feminists, who find the reading of Molly congenial, to the "narratologists," who have reacted to and extended the concept of the arranger. It has also helped spur an interest in a resifting of received ideas, giving rise to some healthy controversy and fresh interpretations. More important, because still relatively new and open to further research, is the virtually untreated question of Joyce's styles, not only his formal tactics, but also the various and rich functions performed by a stylistic vision that aims at the immediacy of gesture.

It is gratifying that much discussion has been generated by the concept of the arranger outlined in these pages. The term has, in fact, become so current and the concept is so frequently alluded to that it is in danger of becoming an unexamined cliché, even though critics as various as Marilyn French, Hugh Kenner, and Shari Benstock have approached the problem with fresh and questioning eyes.

The arranger should be seen as something between a persona and a function, somewhere between the narrator and the implied author. One is tempted to speak of "him" as an "it," kin to Samuel Beckett's Unnamable, but we are also tempted to think of a be-hind-the-scenes persona like the shaper of pantomimes, also called the arranger.[1] Perhaps it would be best to see the arranger as a significant, felt absence in the text, an unstated but inescapable source of control.

More important than the question of identity and locus is the problem of the extent of the arranger's role in *Ulysses*. Already in a *Portrait*, we detect an arranging presence not only in the chapter styles which follow and support the protagonist's growth toward maturity, but also in stylistically distinct interventions like the paratactic opening with its record of infant memories and the dickensian/ibsenian Christmas dinner. Such effects, while necessary to the economy of the text, stand out as products of a force beyond the powers of a malleable narrating persona who is a blend of objective observation, the subjective vision of Stephen, and the boy's own voice and words in free indirect discourse. We may call this dominant narrative method third person personal. It is uniformly applied in the major part of *Portrait* and remains in force as the narrative procedure behind the stream of consciousness effects of the early chapters of *Ulysses*.

This distinction may be crucial to an understanding of the narrative tactics of both books and especially of the limits of the arranging potential. It is, however, at variance with the position advanced by Hugh Kenner in his frequently brilliant and engaging analysis of the arranging process.[2] Kenner would have us push the boundaries of arranging back to the installation of a narrator given to recognizable rhetorical tics like the repetitions of certain key words: *"If her life were a simple rosary of hours, her life simple and strange as a bird's life, gay in the morning, restless all day, tired at sundown? Her heart simple and wilful as a bird's heart?"*[3] The problem raised by this otherwise suggestive position are numerous. If the narrative voice is best seen as a product of the arranging process, where is Joyce's original contribution to fictitional method or where does it properly begin? Writers since Flaubert have consciously constructed voices that were not to be identified with that of the author, and Flaubert's own rhetorical tics are as distinctive as Joyce's: take for example his habit of furnishing his descriptions with participles and other verbals which mobilize stillness.

Kenner's position is that the arranger contributes to the narration in *Ulysses'* opening chapters, supplying rhetorical flourishes and generating a climate of gentle irony for the action. We might agree to turn these obtrusive qualities over to the management of the arranger, letting them constitute a component of the initial mask. However, this would result in a cordoning off of the rhetorically conspicuous component of the scene-setting voice: the affective aspect given over to the registering and heightening of sensation of perception. In this reading, the narrator as a distinct persona or a function resides in two other components or levels of discourse: the pure and transparently objective voice that laconically records routine behavior; the equally bland voice that describes scenes and objects in somewhat more detail. Clearly, both of these help reassure the reader adrift in this strange new medium, this unpredictable narrative space. Both fade with the coming of the late-afternoon and evening hours; neither need be attributed to a capricious arranging presence.

On the other hand, if the more quirky and charming affective voice is seen as an early warning system for the arranging presence, we must also see it as a component of the perceiving character's vision, part of the apparatus that enables us to slip from the outside world into the directly reported thoughtstream, from objective presentation to pure subjectivity. It is consistent with the development of third person subjectivity toward the stream of consciousness by way of free indirect discourse that all three narrative positions are inextricably engaged in a single narrative process.[4] Furthermore, since most of these traits are common to all or most post-flaubertian fiction, and since the sort of manipulation manifested by the arranged passages of *Portrait* and *Ulysses* was innovated by Joyce, the attempt to generalize further the arranged component of the text weakens the concept of arranger. The latter becomes the sum of the narrative process rather than a component of it: the distinction between narrator and arranger is virtually eliminated.

Instead of going that far, we should probably think of the arranging presence as subtly penetrating the fabric of the narrative at a variety of points and in a variety of ways. Intrusion, like the allusive systems, begins long before the reader is aware of any absolute difference between narrative approaches. We find it in the treatment of the initial action of *Ulysses* as seen by an unnamed viewer from an unmarked perspective. It is also behind the phasing-in of stream of consciousness during the cracked mirror paragraph (6), behind the style shifts that mark each of the early chapters, and behind certain manifestations that would otherwise be inexplicable, such as the treatment of Mulligan dressing in "Telemachus" (16–17). Furthermore, the arranger controls the suppression of information and action, an extremely frequent occurrence in the early chapters. Indeed, just about any intrusive or arbitrary phenomenon should be attributed to the arranging persona. We may add that such manipulative procedures usually announce symbolic and thematic resonances while undermining the realistic texture.

Finally, a note on the evolution of the tactic. Recently, in his fine study of the manuscript development, *"Ulysses" in Progress,* Michael Groden has made a case for "Cyclops" as the turning point in the history of the novel's stylistic development.[5] If he is right, we may have to revise our view of the priority if not the significance of the arranger strategy. However, given the *Portrait* as precedent, given the previously drafted chapters and their admittedly less radical but still fairly obvious style changes, and given the fact that other effects ascribed above to the arranger were already in place, it seems unlikely that Joyce did not have in mind some heightening of arbitrariness.[6] Clearly, Joyce had already introduced arranging as a procedure when he began work on "Cyclops." The elaboration of the early chapters had as its consequence the development of a complex narrative strategy which gradually joined the seemingly "objective" narrator with the intrusive and puckish arranging impulse that was destined to take over the narrative functions as the book progressed. Though, as Groden suggests, "Cyclops" (which was followed by the elaboration of "Wandering Rocks" and the introduction of headlines in "Aeolus") may have been a breakthrough, the arranger/narrator interaction seems too fundamental to the overall strategy to have come as a complete afterthought.

Though far from dissatisfied with the view of *Ulysses* presented in these pages, during the last ten years I have had other things to say. In "Stephen on the Rocks," a close reading of one controversial passage in "Proteus" (47–51), I tried to show that what critics have long thought to be a "symbolic" urination by Stephen actually focusses a concealed auto-erotic passage and a latent thematic.[7] The frustrated, hypersensitive solipsist is engaged in what may be his most personal encounter of the book in an interlude that parallels and foreshadows Bloom's masturbation in "Nausikaa" and harks back to and illuminates the famous bird-girl encounter in chapter 4 of *Portrait*. Stephen's behavior, characteristically concealed even from himself, is revealed by a study of his actual movements combined with an analysis of his erotic and anti-erotic musings.

The problems raised by "Cyclops" are more numerous, more complex, and more broadly applicable to the book as a whole. The sudden removal of narrative support, the plunge into an alien sensibility, the objectification of Bloom's experience, and the introduction of the radically intrusive parodic asides all require and reward extended treatment. Actions in this chapter are even more carefully camouflaged than are those of the stream of consciousness chapters or of those passages deliberately obscured by the narrator/arranger procedures. As a result, received opinion saw the context as ominous and sordid, the cast of characters as bibulous, banal, boisterous, and uniformly awed by the chauvinistic citizen, Bloom as heroic against the odds, and the citizen at the center of the action. In fact, the events gleaned from the biased reporting of the gifted mimic and pub raconteur are far more nuanced. My reading reveals a very mixed group of pub-clients evolving toward respectability as the chapter progresses. A concomitant decrease in attention is paid the dropsical old patriot and his patriotic cant. As a consequence, the context becomes less sordid and more commonplace, and the language of the dun is increasingly important as a factor in the generation of mood and attitude. Beyond that, Bloom's preoccupation with Molly and Boylan must be seen as a major factor contributing to his defense of love; the citizen's goading must be seen as the result of his pique at being excluded from both the conversation and the treating.

Until recently, little attention has been paid the physical and temporal circumstances of the chapter's telling, but the temporal references in the text, the rare allusions to current happenings, suggest that the dun is telling the story later in the evening (to an equally nameless listener) in the hope of cadging drinks to sustain his mood. In support of this position, we have a curious and much-studied interlude (335), an entr'acte during which the speaker retreats with us to the water closet, where he indulges in a dual discourse in the present tense, a moment that significantly mediates between the narrated text and the parodic asides, a moment of profound undecidability.[8]

On another level, the parodic asides, written in a variety of late-nineteenth-century popular modes, function as part of an overall strategy that approximates the form of the Dublin Christmas Pantomime, one of Joyce's lasting enthusiasms. Thus "Cyclops" functions as a formal foreshadowing not only of "Oxen of the Sun" but also of "Circe."[9]

Molly, as overheard in "Penelope," is clearly the device Joyce used to bring the pieces of the novel into focus and to resolve the book, if not the action. She is also the presence that dominates Bloom's day through her absence and overshadows all other female presences in this most masculine of texts about two relatively unmasculine males. However, there has been a tendency to confuse the myth of Molly, the bigger-than-life lusting female, earth mother projected by the male imagination and countersigned by Joyce's sub-text, with the woman Joyce actually breathed into recumbent life in the breathless final pages of *Ulysses*.

The "real" Molly, the one Bloom married, the wanton (but calculating) girl who seduced him on the hill of Howth, is an interesting mass of contradictions, partly because she is in an unusual state of mind on the morning of June 17. Not only has she had her first serious encounter with another man, she is also beginning to menstruate, a condition that brings on mood changes and makes it impossible that her intercourse with Boylan will have any consequences. The onset of her period, which occurs toward the middle of the monologue, significantly alters the tone of her discourse and modifies her relationship first to Boylan and then to Bloom.

Molly reveals herself as a somewhat more practical version of Emma Bovary, just as Poldy becomes a more intelligent and vigorous Charles. Her surprise concerning Boylan's sexual capacities is tempered by her disappointment that he is unromantic and boorish. Her defensive criticism of Bloom, with whom she has after all had a limited but not unsatisfactory sexual relationship since the death of Rudy, is tempered by that same romanticism. Poldy, for all his faults, is an imaginative lover and something of a challenge. A review of her life shows us that she has had only a few meagre sexual experiences, including a lesbian interlude on Gibraltar, that she is by no means a star performer, that her Moorish connections are fragile, and that she is essentially cautious. One reason for her recent adventure may be Milly's coming of age, a reminder of her own ageing. Increasingly a source of friction, the growing girl was sent away partly because she threatened to be a rival made in Molly's own image. The Molly who emerges through the monologue is neither completely admirable nor vˊ cious, simply a product of her age and upbringing, less than a victim of Irish mores à la Gerty McDowell, less than liberated, Joyce's partial portrait of Woman.[10]

The ambitious goals Joyce sets himself in the early chapters of *Ulysses,* his need to convey a total daytime consciousness, led him to improvise and update all manner of tactics and devices. We have read as much about his epiphanies as about his stream of consciousness techniques and the nature and uses of his style. However, little progress has been made in defining the precise role of the epiphanies (moments of heightened awareness, secular illuminations) as an expressive and formal device in either *Portrait* or *Ulysses.* Key passages in the *Portrait* contain examples of the pure joycean epiphany: the three-part sequence beginning repeatedly with the phrase "He was sitting . . ." (*Portrait,* 66-70), the tight-knit opening passage composed of nothing but memory nuggets (*Portrait,* 7-8), and the concluding diary which at times seems to be compounded of unassimilated epiphanic perceptions (*Portrait,* 247-52). In *Ulysses,* we may note instances scattered throughout the opening pages and contributing importantly to a character's view of self and world as, for example, in Stephen's dream vision of his mother: "Silently, in a dream she had come to him after her death, her wasted body within its loose brown graveclothes giving off an odour of wax and rosewood, her breath, that had bent upon him, mute, reproachful, a faint odour of wetted ashes" (5). There is no question that Joyce made frequent and significant use of such vivid instants, and it is probable that he used many which have not survived in existing collections of the manuscripts. We can surmise that they were used fairly systematically, and from the evidence, we may gather that they contributed greatly to the extraordinary density and precision of expression evident in the early chapters of *Ulysses*. Beyond that, it is worth noting that Joyce continued to collect intense or revealing moments. His notebooks for *Finnegans Wake* contain a good number of them even though the *Wake* was not an apt vehicle for this essentially realistic tool.

Composition of place is of a very different nature, though it too is a device christened by Joyce himself and taken from theology. St. Ignatius Loyola prescribed composition of place in his *Spiritual Exercises* as the first contemplative step, the conjuring up of a setting for the object of veneration. Joyce lets Stephen apply the term to a radically different but parallel procedure by which he imagines circumstantial content for an action he has not witnessed, such as the behavior of Shakespeare described in "Scylla and Charybdis" (186). The device comes to prominence long before it is mentioned, informing the retreat sermons of chapter 3 in *Portrait*. It is applied by Stephen unwittingly in his reactions to those sermons and later, more consciously, in his diary entries on Cranly's father and E.C. at home (*Portrait*, 248, 249).

In *Ulysses*, composition of place is used consciously and unconsciously by Stephen and Bloom. We see it in the Oxford ragging episode beginning "Young shouts of moneyed voices . . ." (7) where it is generated by the narrating presence. Stephen himself uses it in transforming the two women on the beach at the beginning of "Proteus" first into midwives and then into the heroines of his "Parable of the Plums." The procedure is simple. Stephen first sees and then develops a profile and context for one of two "*Frauenzimmer*": "From the liberties, out for the day. Mrs Florence MacCabe, relict of the late Patk MacCabe, deeply lamented, of Bride Street. One of her sisterhood lugged me squealing into life" (37). The process continues in "Aeolus," where Stephen places the same ladies in the middle of Dublin to perform a mock fertility ritual on the top of Nelson's pillar. Just as we have had a chance to follow the development of this image, watching the associations accumulate, composition of place reveals the imagination at work on worldly but unwitnessed events, generating fictions that help furnish the protagonist's universe and reflect hidden motivations.

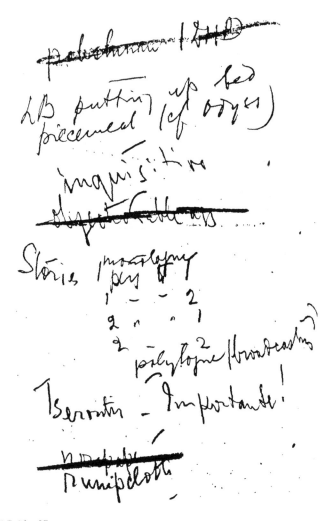

VI.B.10 — 37

Pages from Notebook VI.B.10 (James Joyce Archive Volume 31, pages 97 and 122) containing allusions to the behavior of Stephen and Bloom and a suggestive schema for Point of View.

They have yet to be fully studied, but it would not be surprising if such a study would lead us straight to "Circe," the ultimate in imaginary space to which most of *Ulysses* contributes and in which the arranger is the master of meditation.[11]

Among the most intriguing and disturbing features of *Ulysses* are discontinuities like the abrupt style changes that punctuate each chapter, the intrusions that mark the arranger's presence in "Scylla and Charybdis," "Wandering Rocks," and "Cyclops," and the juxtaposed questions and answers in "Ithaca." Such passages and others, smaller in magnitude but no less striking, have been noted but never fully studied or explained. Like so much else in *Ulysses*, they can best be understood in relation to *Portrait*, where we first note the use of the device I am calling parataxis, the grammatical form which omits proper coordination and subordination and boldly juxtaposes fragments of discourse. In *Portrait*, parataxis is present on all levels (see the abrupt transitions, the changes in style between and within chapters, and the frequent use of associative linkage). However, the most startling use of discontinuity occurs in the opening and closing sections which are also the most revolutionary aspects of the book. Thus, the early memories are presented to us without mediation in a crude list which is only gradually revealed to be chronological, an actual record of time passing in the past tense. The reader is immediately obliged to fill in gaps, establish contexts, and justify a revolutionary strategy. This accomplished, he is ready for anything else the book offers in the way of stylistic oddities and discontinuities. Beyond that, we may see in the coincidence of opening and closing discontinuities an emblem of the process of birth, the rebirth of the "soul," signaling the cyclical nature not only of Stephen's development but of the book as a chapter in that development.

Though ultimately more radical, the parataxis in *Ulysses* is initially less striking. Birth and rebirth, for all their desperate circularity, are more hopeful and more appropriate to romantic youth than to the jaded comic universe of mature *Dublin*. The most striking instances of disruption occur in the middle of the book in "Wandering Rocks" and especially in "Sirens." The overture of that chapter is paratactic both in its radical juxtaposition of disparate phrases and sentences and retrospectively in its yoking together of incongruous elements from the chapter to come. Though the question is too complex to be dealt with here,[12] we may summarize briefly the varieties and functions of *Ulysses'* paratactics.

In the opening chapters, where order is dictated by the clarity of the daylight, if not the quality of the protagonists' thought, arbitrary conjunctions occur mainly on the micro-structural level. The narrative and stream of consciousness techniques emphasize an associative logic and dictate the suppression of naturalistic details during moments of intense thought. Frequently, passages resolve themselves into random-seeming lists for which the reader must supply the logic, as when Stephen reacts to Mr Deasy's praise of the Protestant Orangemen's role in Irish history: "Glorious, pious and immortal memory. The lodge of Diamond in Armagh the splendid behung with corpses of papishes. Hoarse, masked and armed, the planters' covenant. The black north and true blue bible. Croppies lie down" (31). Here, the skeletal fragments gain in force by what they do not contain, the implied action of the missing verbs. Such gaps signify.

With the increasingly obvious arranger intervention come broader if not more effective tactics. But with the broader tactics comes a diminishing attention to detail and nuance on the level of action. As a result, disruption in the later chapters is ultimately less confusing than the proliferation of disjunct details in the early ones. The parodic catalogues in "Cyclops" demand relatively little concentration and reflection, though they may impede the action and still time. The uproarious conclusion to "Oxen of the Sun," like the chapter as a whole with its jostling styles, is less an intellectual challenge than a challenge to remove the screens imposed on action by presentation. The reader becomes the object of the text's activity, and the engagement is with the text as experience, while the protagonists' predicaments are rendered universal by the style. Where formerly paratactic juxtaposition helped condense, here the same device, differently handled, serves to inflate the human circumstance supplying effects that delight, divert, confuse, and dismay in the name of an overarching unity of purpose: the presentation of a universal but uniformly human predicament. It is fitting therefore that the most systematically paratactic chapter, the catechistic "Ithaca," which pitilessly deconstructs the moment of contact between Stephen and Bloom, conveys tedium rather than outrage and confusion and that the reader's impulse is to weed out the accumulated verbiage as much as to supply the missing items. That is, despite the revelatory details, the items we search for in this haystack are clues to the nature of a richly evocative human encounter which may in fact have the dimensions of that proverbial needle. Significantly, Molly's coda, the tale that seems to wag the book, is so presented as to mask its essential confusion. Yet, as befits unfocussed discourse, the wanderings of a mind free of almost all external constraints and unbound by logic, her monologue is characterized by unfinished sentences, false linkages, and logical leaps. Though by no means uniform, the muted parataxis of the concluding chapters reverses the thrust of the early chapters, providing a perverse balance for their more vital profusion and confusion, but there is throughout a careful balancing of paratactic and hypotactic effects.

Sorting through the many books on *Ulysses* published during the last decade, we are struck by three relatively fresh tendencies. The first is scholarly: the production of manuscript editions, genetic studies, critical tools, and reference books. The second is critical: in a variety of studies attention is being paid to the givens of the text, to details of action obfuscated by style or simply omitted, to the nature and predicament of the characters, and to the quality and nature of the styles and language. In short, there is much interest in *how Ulysses* means as opposed to particular aspects of *what* it may mean, in the signifying process rather than in anyone's version of significance. With that, one hopes, will come a greater sensitivity to the dynamics of the book and to the aesthetic accomplishment, the joys of Joyce. A third and more theoretical tendency is illustrated by books like Wolfgang Iser's *The Implied Reader* and Dorrit Cohn's *Transparent Minds,* both of which try to fit Joyce into a larger theoretical context.

With the publication of the Rosenbach materials and the more copious and perhaps more authoritative materials in *The James Joyce Archive,* we now have all that is needed to establish a definitive text of *Ulysses.* We also have, in the manuscripts themselves and in the early notes, a treasury awaiting critics with vision. Following Jack P. Dalton's lead, Hans Gabler has begun work on his much-publicized computer project designed to weed out the startling number of errors, ranging from punctuation to omitted phrases that have crept into the texts we all use. There can be no question that without such improvements, close reading, which for good reasons is more than ever common, is at risk.

Editions and studies of the manuscripts are becoming increasingly numerous and sophisticated. Following the work of Walton Litz, who synthesized an enormous amount of material to give an account of the evolution of both *Ulysses* and *Finnegans Wake,* we have Phillip Herring's annotated editions of the notesheets, drafts, and notebooks and Michael Groden's remarkable account of crucial moments in the development of *Ulysses.* Critics have begun drawing upon these studies for evidence, but they are only beginning to develop creative approaches to the manuscript materials.

Among the volumes following in the wake of Weldon Thorton's study of joycean allusions, we have Gifford and Seidman's compendious and occasionally mistaken *Notes for "Ulysses,"* John Henry Raleigh's useful but equally flawed *Chronicle of Leopold and Molly Bloom,* an attempt at fictional historiography, and Clive Hart and Leo Knuth's useful and accurate *Topographical Guide.* More recently, Bernard and Shari Benstock have produced their account of all the characters in the book. Though potentially helpful, such books, like the earlier plot summaries, should be used with caution.

There is a new scholarly turn of mind in Joyce criticism, a tendency that can be traced partly to Robert Martin Adams's distress at discovering missing threads in Joyce's naturalistic fabric, partly from *Finnegans Wake* scholarship. C. H. Peake's *James Joyce: The Citizen and the Artist* attempts (rather longwindedly) to give a commonsense reading for beginning students. Paul P. J. van Caspel's meticulous Dutch dissertation, *Bloomers on the Liffey: Eisegetical Readings of James Joyce's "Ulysses" Part II,* takes on a generous selection of critics and translators, while giving a corrective reading of the central chapters of *Ulysses.* Van Caspel is particularly good on the errors of the plot summarizers and annotators. The result is salutory, and one hopes that his book will get the attention it deserves.

Like the weather, style in *Ulysses* is something everybody talks about. Most of our studies do more with the "function" of styles than with their nature or with Joyce's language as an expressive medium. But in 1973, we saw the appearance of Anthony Burgess' breezy and quirky *Joysprick: an Introduction to the Language of James Joyce* and Erwin R. Steinberg's determinedly wrongheaded but occasionally useful *The Stream of Consciousness and Beyond in "Ulysses."* More recently Roy K. Gottfried has published a study of the underlying joycean idiom which should stimulate further studies.

Of a more general nature, though they touch upon styles and stylistics, are Marilyn French's level-headed and perceptive reading of the book as a map of the human predicament, *The Book as World,* Hugh Kenner's suggestive and often brilliant *"Ulysses,"* Elliot B. Gose, Jr.'s *The Transformation Process in "Ulysses,"* and James H. Maddox, Jr.'s *Joyce's "Ulysses" and the Assault upon Character.* All of these books are useful if not seminal. All of them point up an essential quality of Joyce's works, a polyvalence which sanctions readings that can be complementary even when they seem contradictory but which leaves us with a sense that what has been said is at once too little and too much.

There are also a variety of more limited approaches, source studies, thematic analyses, biographical approaches, a few of which are listed in the bibliography along with some of the many collections of essays. Of the latter we should single out *James Joyce's "Ulysses": Critical Essays* which features original readings of the eighteen chapters by eighteen critics. Among the most frequently cited of all Joyce books, this volume may have the staying power of Sean Givens' classic *James Joyce: Two Decades of Criticism.*

Though we now have two psychoanalytic studies and one special issue of the *James Joyce Quarterly* devoted to psychoanalysis, we await full-length theoretical treatments by marxist, structuralist, and reader response critics, studies which willy-nilly will come, along with books by writers with other fixed theoretical biases. This is assured as much by the growing interest in theory in the United States as by the growing interest in Joyce by the French, Germans, Italians, and Spanish. This interest, plus a number of recent translations and a wave of increasingly able Joyce-influenced novels in many languages, is one of the most promising signs for Joyce studies. In the future there is bound to be more dialogue among cultures and a wider range of approaches to a book that is now accessible not only to college undergraduates but also the casual reader with a good ear and a ready wit.

Appendices

Notes

Bibliography

Index

Appendix I
Plot Summary

Ulysses: a rough but perhaps adequate summary of the goings and comings, acts and reactions, recorded and shaped in the eighteen chapters of *Ulysses.*

1. "Telemachus" (pp. 2–23): Stephen Dedalus, once more in Ireland but still displaced, watches as the medical student, Buck Mulligan, with whom he shares his Martello tower lodgings, cavorts and shaves in the morning sunlight on the tower's roof. In a brief discussion Stephen complains about the nighttime raving of their new roommate, the English hibernophile Haines. He also reproaches Mulligan for having affronted his pride by commenting wryly on the death of May Dedalus. They go down into the living area where Mulligan prepares and Stephen helps serve a breakfast interrupted by the appearance of the old milk woman who must be paid. After breakfast Mulligan first dresses and then, having walked to the nearby swimming area, disrobes, asking the departing Stephen to leave behind the key to the tower. They are to meet at 12:30 at the Ship pub, where they will begin spending the money Stephen is to receive for his work as a teacher. Time: 8:00 a.m.

2. "Nestor" (pp. 24–35): At Mr. Deasy's school for Protestant boys, Stephen teaches an inattentive and puzzled class lessons in history and literature before the hockey break at the end of the short Thursday session. One boy, Sargent, with whose graceless self Stephen identifies his own youth, stays behind for special tutoring in math. The second half of the chapter shows Stephen once again in the role of pupil. He receives, along with his salary, a lecture from Mr. Deasy on thrift and Irish history, and an example of intolerance to which he openly objects. Before leaving, he also receives a letter on hoof and mouth disease which he promises to deliver to the newspapers. Time: 10:00 a.m.

3. "Proteus" (pp. 37–51): Alone and aimless, apparently killing time before going to meet Mulligan and Haines, Stephen walks the beach at Sandymount, not far from the place where he encountered the birdgirl emblem of his new-found freedom in chapter 4 of *A Portrait of the Artist.* There he sees two women walk to the water and tests Aristotle's theory of

139

perception as he himself wanders in the direction of his Uncle Richie's house. Lost in meditation, he passes his destination and decides instead to rest on a rock where, inspired by a pair of cockle-pickers, he writes a brief and derivative poem and guiltily indulges in erotic fantasies. The homeric theme of change invests the language of this chapter as well as its development. Time: 11:00 a.m.

4. "Calypso" (pp. 54–70): We are introduced to Leopold Bloom, a Jewish/Irish canvasser for newspaper ads who plays Odysseus to Stephen's Telemachus. During this chapter he leaves home briefly to buy a pork kidney for his breakfast from a Jewish butcher, and returns to find the mail, part of which he delivers to his bedwarm wife, Molly, to whom he also serves her breakfast. The letters include one from his daughter, Milly, working at Mullingar as a photographer's assistant, and a note for Molly from her impresario and future lover Blazes Boylan. After eating his (burnt) kidney, Bloom relieves himself in the outhouse before leaving the house for the day, keyless and dressed in mourning for Paddy Dignam's funeral. Time: 8:00 a.m.

5. "Lotuseaters" (pp. 71–86): Killing time before the funeral, Bloom picks up an amorous letter from "Martha Clifford" under his pseudonym Henry Flower at the Westland Row post office. Before he can read the letter, he is waylaid by McCoy, whose conversation gives him a chance to indulge his voyeuristic tendencies. Alone at last, he reads the letter from Martha before entering a church where he observes the service with comic critical distance. On leaving the church, he meets Bantam Lyons, to whom he hands his newspaper with what the latter takes as a tip to bet on the horse Throwaway. The *far niente* theme shapes this chapter's language. Time: 10:00 a.m.

6. "Hades" (pp. 87–115): Bloom joins Simon Dedalus, Cunningham, and Power for a carriage ride to Glasnevin cemetery, where they commune with ghosts of the Irish and personal past and witness the burial of Paddy Dignam. There Bloom encounters the reporter Hynes, who questions him concerning an unknown man in a macintosh coat; he also speaks with the convert Kernan and is snubbed by the attorney John Henry Menton, an admirer of Molly's charms. The real action is in the often hilarious mental play of Bloom faced with the false piety induced by the context. Time: 11:00 a.m.

7. "Aeolus" (pp. 116–50): Negotiating over an advertisement for a grocer named Keyes, Bloom visits the offices of his newspaper. When he has finished behind the scenes, he enters the front office, where we find congregated the first of several groups of symposiasts. Simon Dedalus, the sponge Lenehan, Professor MacHugh, and the editor Myles Crawford (a

figure for Aeolus), among others in a changing cast, are discussing orators, rhetoric, and journalistic history. Bloom's dealings with Crawford and his client Keyes recede to form the backdrop for the conversation in one of several joycean attempts to suggest synchronous activity. When Simon leaves, Stephen appears with his letter and, after some banter (and the offer of a job), leads all to a pub. Bloom, returning from Keyes's store, is given the cold shoulder by a thirsty editor at the very moment that Stephen is telling his "Parable of the Plums" to a shifting and uncomprehending audience. In every possible way, this chapter is appropriately windblown; it is rendered even more arbitrary in appearance by the intrusive headings. Time: 12:00 noon.

8. "Lestrygonians" (pp. 151–83): It is lunchtime and Bloom roams the streets searching for a satisfactory place to eat. Though he meets an old flame, Josie Breen, and sees a rich variety of sights while rejecting various eating places, the action of this chapter is, like that of "Proteus," largely mental. The snack he eats at Davy Byrne's "moral" pub puts him in contact with several Dublin characters, including an "admiring" Nosey Flynn, and gives us our first glimpse of Irish pub-life. The action ends as Bloom ducks into the National Gallery to avoid Boylan. This chapter abounds in oblique references to crude eating, food, and even cannibalism. Time: 1:00 p.m.

9. "Scylla and Charybdis" (pp. 184–218): While Bloom is in the gallery, Stephen holds forth across the courtyard in the National Library, where he has come to deliver the Deasy letter to the Theosophist AE (George Russell) and perhaps to intercept Mulligan and Haines. In this, the second of our symposia, he is expounding his theory concerning the relationship of Shakespeare to his play *Hamlet* to the assembled literati. Though he makes every effort to impress and convince, once again he finds an inattentive and deeply uncomprehending, if not hostile, audience. The aristotelian John Eglinton, the editor of *Dana*, to whom he wishes to sell his literary output is particularly unreceptive. Halfway through the long, convoluted, and ultimately very personal argument, AE leaves, only to be replaced by Mulligan, whose entrance disorients Stephen. In stealing attention, Mulligan paradoxically saves his "friend" from worse embarrassment and confusion and facilitates his exit. Bloom, bent on researching the Keyes ad, flits through this chapter as a background presence. The chapter is peppered with curious asides generated by the arranger/narrator who, beginning with the "Aeolus" headlines, has begun to infiltrate and darken the text. Time: 2:00 p.m.

10. "Wandering Rocks" (pp. 219–55): This pedestrian (in more than one sense), central, and mediating chapter is divided into nineteen brief

passages treating events occurring in different parts of Dublin and laced together by means of intrusive references to simultaneous activities. (One sees here further evidence of the arranging presence.) It opens with an account of Stephen's former mentor's (Father Conmee's) trip across town on an errand of mercy for Dignam's widow; it closes with the progress of a viceregal procession to the opening of the Mirus Bazaar (see chapter 13 or "Nausikaa"). Thus it joins the city under the ironically presented protection of Church and State. Though the case is large, the events themselves are small, and Bloom and Stephen are lost in the motion of the blocks of action that are being displaced in space and time. They appear only briefly in the central segments and are not among those listed as "witnesses" to the procession. In this chapter Blazes Boylan is addressed over the telephone and is seen buying a gift basket for Molly. Time: 3:00 p.m.

11. "Sirens" (pp. 256-91): This chapter is mockingly cast in the form of a fugue. After the long overture of disjunct fragments drawn from the process of the narrative, Bloom follows Blazes Boylan into the Ormond Hotel Bar and Restaurant on the Liffey river quay. There Boylan pauses briefly to flirt with the barmaids and to place a bet through Lenehan on the horse Sceptre before keeping (belatedly) his appointment with Molly. Unwilling or unable to follow him and half resigned to his new condition, Bloom stays on for lunch with Richie Goulding while, in another room, a group that includes Simon Dedalus and Ben Dollard sings sentimental favorites. After lunch, Bloom wanders off, carefully releasing a final fizzle of fart to the sound of band music. Much of the chapter's action concerns the "seductive" wiles of the two barmaids, who compete with the vocal music, and the absent allure of Molly to suggest the presence of sirens in a chapter which, through its disjunct style and "fugal" form, captures the quality of the various actions occurring simultaneously in parts of the hotel and town. Time: circa 4:00 p.m.

12. "Cyclops" (pp. 292-345): In Barney Kiernan's pub near the law courts an ill-assorted group gathers (apparently if not actually) around an over-the-hill Irish patriot, self-styled the "citizen." The narrative is in the voice of a bitter and sardonic barfly who earns his living by collecting "bad and doubtful debts" and who seems to be telling his tale some hours after the events to a patient treater. (Hence the chapter may well have a double temporality suggestive of another sort of simultaneity. It describes at 9 p.m. what occurred at 5 p.m., dealing with the narrative process as well as the tale.) The narrative is periodically interrupted by parodic asides in other voices controlled by the arranging presence and putting the narrator's account to the foil. This is the third of the symposium chapters and, like the others, complex in its plot, however trivial the events them-

selves may be. Bloom unwillingly and all too soberly takes part in an increasingly drunken and irrational argument whose apparent focus is nationalism. He has come to meet Martin Cunningham and two others on an errand of mercy to Dignam's widow and, because he is distracted over Molly's behavior with Boylan, finds himself taking unpopular positions against the anti-semitic citizen. There are several key moments in the action proper. One occurs when, after defending Love as a virtue over Hate, Bloom absents himself briefly. Another occurs when the narrator goes to relieve himself during the succeeding attack and half-hearted defense of Bloom. During the latter's absence, Lenehan, bitter at having lost at the races, claims that Bloom is picking up his winnings on the horse Throwaway. This leads to a final contretemps when Bloom fails to buy the round of drinks expected by the citizen, who then launches a violent but ineffectual assault to which Bloom clumsily but openly responds as he is whisked away by an embarrassed Cunningham and friends. Time: 5:00 p.m. (action) and perhaps 9:00 p.m. (narration as action).

13. "Nausikaa" (pp. 346–82): The scene is Sandymount strand, where Stephen meditated in "Proteus" at 11:00 a.m., but the voice that speaks the first half of this episode is that of a consumer or producer of female pulp fiction, and the chief protagonist is a young woman slipping into spinsterhood and stimulated by the onset of menstruation. Gerty MacDowell is at the beach with some girlfriends, one of whom, the tomboyish Cissy Caffrey, is minding her baby brothers. The narrator of this saccharine monologue gives an account not only of what transpires on the beach (very little), but also of Gerty's background, life, aspirations, and reflections. The account, interspersed with a description of a temperance retreat taking place at a nearby church, culminates in the fireworks display at the Mirus Bazaar toward which the viceregal procession was wending at the end of "Wandering Rocks" (see again church vs. state). The public display is countered by Gerty's silent flirtation with a dark stranger sitting opposite her on the beach. When the narrative vantage point shifts from Gerty to the voyeur, we join a grateful Bloom in his postmasturbatory reflections as he contemplates the departing girl (she limps, being lame) and begins to write a message in the sand before permitting himself to doze off as had Stephen in the famous conclusion to chapter 4 of *Portrait*. Time: 8:00 p.m.

14. "Oxen of the Sun" (pp. 383–428): The scene is below stairs in the Hollis Street lying-in hospital where Mina Purefoy is experiencing a difficult birth. Bloom, still unable to return home for fear of meeting Boylan and confirming his suspicions, is paying a late-night sympathy call. Here, as in "Cyclops," he is drawn into an alien context (our final

symposium), invited, that is, to share the company of a group of carousing wits. In that group is Stephen Dedalus, who, still undecided about where he will spend the night, has come in search of Mulligan and Haines. The action of this chapter is more than ever a matter of style and presentation, specifically of the historical development of English prose styles which serve to describe in a frequently opaque but always amusing manner the conversation of the youths, a thunderstorm, the arrival of Mulligan and Haines, and even the reactions of a displaced and increasingly uncomfortable Bloom. When the baby is finally delivered and the young intern, for whom the rest are waiting, is free to leave, the young men, followed by Bloom, walk to a pub where they drink till closing time, treated perhaps by Stephen. The language of the closing pages, a confused babble of jargons, not only obscures the action; it also reveals, however obliquely, much that we did not know about the narrative circumstances as they relate to Bloom and Stephen. Time: 10:00 p.m.

15. "Circe" (pp. 429–609): After an altercation with Mulligan, Stephen takes Lynch with him to Nighttown, where he hopes to see a whore whose father is a Protestant minister. Bloom, who is by now interested in the fate and well-being of this drunken and vulnerable young man, follows him into the hallucinatory atmosphere, locating him at the house of Bella Cohen. There he meets the whore Zoe, is briefly mesmerized by the appearance of the whoremistress, and watches as Stephen first plays the piano and then dances himself into a drunken fury during which he attacks and dents a mauve lampshade. Bloom, who has taken care to relieve Stephen of what remains of his salary, pays the damages to Bella Cohen before rushing out, too late to prevent Stephen from being knocked unconscious by a drunken British tommy with whom he is having a one-sided metaphysical argument. With the help of the funeral director Corny Kelleher, Bloom protects Stephen from the police and then watches over his body. We have given thus far only the barest outline of a chapter written in the forms of an expressionistic/faustian drama. Since the true "action" takes place on another level in the blurred awarenesses of Bloom and Stephen, "Circe" is very hard to summarize. To begin with, the entire context is blurred by hallucinatory effects which infect even the reader's awareness. But the source of the most outrageous and hilarious fantasies is Bloom's subconscious, where psychodramas begin to be acted out with his appearance on the scene. A string of such imaginary experiences punctuated by brief moments of lucidity eventuate in his snapping out of his fatigue-induced stupor and attending to Stephen's increasingly strange behavior. In the process, Bloom has been (subconsciously) exposed to the fears that cloud his mind and have darkened his day. It is this cathartic ex-

posure that may release him to perform further actions and to face his future. His hallucinations are mainly discreet, but the text prepares us for shared visions, and Bloom's liberation coincides with Stephen's loss of control. In an explosion of activity during which private horrors are made searingly public, the youth acts out an encounter with his mother's ghost and lashes out against the light before he converses with the figures of king and country standing ghastly behind the soldier. After the rescue of Stephen, Bloom imagines that he sees rising from the recumbent form the ghost of his son Rudy, dead eleven years earlier at the age of eleven days. Thus he completes the paternal identification hinted at throughout the book. Time: 12:00 midnight.

16. "Eumeus" (pp. 612-65): After Stephen has revived, Bloom escorts him to a cabman's shelter run by the reputed ex-Invincible, Skin-the-goat. On the way there Stephen is accosted by a down-and-outer named Corley, whom he sardonically advises to apply for the job at Deasy's school. Once in the shelter, the two wanderers listen to the complicated lies of a returning sailor before Bloom, who has shown Stephen a photo of Molly, leads him off for more refreshments and a bed at number 7 Eccles Street. This chapter, during which the men presumably ge to know each other, is told in a tired and clotted prose by a bloomish narrator who conveys the fact that neither man fully understands the other. On the other hand, it shows us a Stephen who is more open than we would expect and a Bloom more capable of positive action. Time: 1:00 a.m.

17. "Ithaca" (pp. 666-737): Having forgotten his key in the morning, Bloom is obliged to climb the areaway railing to let Stephen into his house, where he serves him cocoa with cream and exchanges information and reminiscences before offering to put him up for the night. After Stephen's (polite/curt) refusal, the two men go into the back garden, where both urinate under the stars, and Stephen departs to the sound of church bells. Reentering his house, Bloom discovers that the furniture has been moved, contemplates his future with an adulterous Molly, and goes through the contents of a drawer full of records of his/their past before climbing the stairs to join Molly in bed. In his kitchen he has found a jar of Plumtree's Potted Meat. In his bed he finds crumbs from that jar left by Boylan. But he has already made his peace with his new condition and has even generated in his mind a list of other possible (previous) lovers. Lying in bed, his head to her feet, he recounts a censored version of his day and asks for breakfast in bed before dropping off to sleep. Here again the tactics of the chapter are as significant as the action itself. As if to imitate the chaos in Odysseus' halls, the text breaks down into a catechism in which even the most trivial detail is magnified while some of the more significant are omit-

ted, a device that turns the two main protagonists into items in a crowded inventory and their drama into an intergalactic one. Time: 2:00 a.m.

18. "Penelope" (pp. 738-83): The cool prose of "Ithaca" is followed by the bedwarmed verbal flow of Molly. Though she has been a presence throughout the book in the minds of Bloom and others, she takes on real dimensions only when her voice can be heard. Her monologue, divided into eight unpunctuated segments, begins with a reaction to Bloom's request for breakfast, continues with a celebration of the afternoon of "love" with Boylan, then proceeds to review her marriage, her girlhood on Gibraltar, her various infatuations, and her dreams of future romance before returning, by way of a desire for young lovers and specifically the young "poet" Stephen, to an equivocal but curiously emphatic acceptance of the young Bloom who resides still in the older man beside her. The only action properly speaking is the trip she makes to her chamberpot, where she discovers that she has gotten her period. Time: unspecified but probably 3:00-4:00 a.m.

Appendix II
Joyce's Schema

Author's note: I have corrected obvious spelling errors and regularized Joyce's punctuation while maintaining his spelling of proper names even when it is at variance with my own.

Title	Scene	Hour	Organ	Art
I TELEMACHIA				
1 Telemachus	The Tower	8 a.m.		theology
2 Nestor	The School	10 a.m.		history
3 Proteus	The Strand	11 a.m.		philology
II ODYSSEY				
1 Calypso	The House	8 a.m.	kidney	economics
2 Lotuseaters	The Bath	10 a.m.	genitals	botany, chemistry
3 Hades	The Grave-yard	11 a.m.	heart	religion
4 Eolus	The News-paper	12 noon	lungs	rhetoric
5 Lestry-gonians	The Lunch	1 p.m.	esophagus	architecture
6 Scylla and Charybdis	The Library	2 p.m.	brain	literature
7. Wandering Rocks	The Streets	3 p.m.	blood	mechanics
8 Sirens	The Concert Room	4 p.m.	ear	music
9 Cyclops	The Tavern	5 p.m.	muscle	politics
10 Nausikaa	The Rocks	8 p.m.	eye, nose	painting
11 Oxen of Sun	The Hospital	10 p.m.	womb	medicine
12 Circe	The Brothel	12 midnight	locomotor apparatus	magic
III NOSTOS				
1 Eumeus	The Shelter	1 a.m.	nerves	navigation
2 Ithaca	The House	2 a.m.	skeleton	science
3 Penelope	The Bed		flesh	

Colour	Symbol	Technic	Correspondence
white gold	heir	narrative (young)	(Stephen—Telemachus, Hamlet: Buck Mulligan—Antinous: Milkwoman—Mentor)
brown	horse	catechism (personal)	(Deasy—Nestor: Pisistratus—Sargent: Helen—Mrs O'Shea)
green	tide	monologue (male)	(Proteus—Primal Matter: Kevin Egan—Menelaus: Megapenthus—The Cocklepicker)
orange	nymph	narrative (mature)	(Calypso—The Nymph: Dlugacz—The Recall: Zion—Ithaca)
	eucharist	narcissism	(Lotuseaters—Cabhorses, Communicants, Soldiers, Eunuchs, Bather, Watchers of Cricket)
white black	caretaker	incubism	(Dodder, Grand and Royal Canals, Liffey—The 4 Rivers: Cunningham—Sisyphus: Father Coffey—Cerberus: Caretaker—Hades: Daniel O'Connell—Hercules: Dignam—Elpenor: Parnell—Agamemnon: Menton—Ajax)
red	editor	enthymemic	(Crawford—Eolus: Incest—Journalism: Floating Island—Press)
	constables	peristalsis	(Antiphates—Hunger: The Decoy—Food: Lestrygonians—Teeth)
	Stratford, London	dialectic	(The Rock—Aristotle, Dogma—Stratford: The Whirlpool—Plato, Mysticism, London: Ulysses—Socrates, Jesus, Shakespeare)
	citizens	labyrinth	(Bosphorus—Liffey: European bank—Viceroy: Asiatic bank—Conmee: Symplegades—Groups of Citizens)
	barmaids	fuga per canonem	(Sirens—Barmaids: Isle—Bar)
	fenian	gigantism	(Noman—I: Stake—Cigar: Challenge—Apotheosis)
grey, blue	virgin	tumescence detumescence	(Phaeacia—Star of the Sea: Gerty—Nausikaa)
white	mothers	embryonic development	(Hospital—Trinacria: Lampetie, Phaethusa—Nurses: Helios—Horne: Oxen—Fertility:Crime—Fraud)
	whore	hallucination	(Circe—Bella)
	sailors	narrative (old)	(Eumeus—Skin the Goat: Sailor—Ulysses Pseudangelos: Melanthius—Corley)
	comets	catechism (impersonal)	(Eurymachus—Boylan: Suitors—Scruples: Bow—Reason)
	earth	monologue (female)	(Penelope—Earth: Web—Movement)

Appendix III

Chronology

1882 Birth of James Aloysius Joyce in Dublin on February 2.
On May 6 the Invincibles commit the Phoenix Park murders in Dublin.

1888–91 Joyce attends Clongowes Wood School.
Parnell's trials and death (1890–91).
Symbolism blooms in France (1886–98).

1893–98 Joyce attends Belvedere College.
Trials of Oscar Wilde (1895).
Rise and fall of aestheticism.

1898–1902 Joyce attends University College.
W. B. Yeats's *The Countess Cathleen* becomes a storm center for the Irish literary theatre (1899).
The Dreyfus affair rocks France (Zola's *J'accuse,* 1898).
Sigmund Freud formulates his major psychoanalytic theories.

1902–4 Paris and return. Death of his mother (August 13, 1903). Departure with Nora Barnacle into exile: Pola, Trieste.
Yeats, Moore, Lady Gregory, and AE active in the Irish literary renaissance.
Russo-Japanese War (1904).

1909–12 Two trips to Dublin: to found a cinema and to push the publication of *Dubliners.*
The period of German expressionism and of Picasso's and Braque's experiments with cubism.

1914 Publication of *Dubliners* by Grant Richards in London. Serial publication of *A Portrait of the Artist as a Young Man* begins in *The Egoist.*
World War I.

1915 Move to Zurich.
Einstein announces his general theory of relativity (1913–16).

151

1916–17   Publication of *A Portrait of the Artist as a Young Man* by B. W. Huebsch in New York.
          Easter rebellion in Dublin (1916)
          Start of the Russian Revolution on October 25, 1917.

1918   Publication of *Exiles* by Grant Richards in London. Serial publication of *Ulysses* begins in *The Little Review*. Harriet Weaver becomes his Maecenas.
          World War I ends on November 11.

1920   Joyce moves with his family from Trieste to Paris.
          The Government of Ireland Act establishes separate parliaments for North and South (rejected by the South).

1922   *The Little Review* is prosecuted in America for the publication of parts of *Ulysses*. Publication of *Ulysses* by Sylvia Beach in Paris.
          The Irish Free State is proclaimed.

1927   Serial publication of *Finnegans Wake* begins in *transition*.
          Joyce is the silent center of a new movement in Paris.
          Surrealism flourishes in France.

1933   The lifting of the ban permits publication of *Ulysses* in America.
          Hitler named Reichschancellor on January 30.

1939   Publication of *Finnegans Wake* by Faber and Faber in London and Viking Press in New York.
          World War II begins after invasion of Poland on September 1.

1941   Death in Zurich on January 13.

Notes

Chapter I: Backgrounds

1 *Ulysses* (New York: Random House, 1961). All page references in the text are to this edition. No current edition of *Ulysses* is completely reliable, but the errors are not apt to distract the general reader.

2 *Finnegans Wake* (New York: Viking Press, 1939), p. 288.

3 Richard Ellmann, *James Joyce* (New York: Oxford University Press, 1965), p. 10.

4 See *A Portrait of the Artist as a Young Man* (New York: Viking Press, 1964), p. 165.

5 For a balanced discussion of Joyce's traiing, see Kevin Sullivan, *Joyce Among the Jesuits* (New York: Columbia University Press, 1958).

6 For earlier versions and a succinct discussion, see Richard Ellmann and Ellsworth Mason, eds., James Joyce, *The Critical Writings* (New York: Viking Press, 1959), pp. 141–48 and *passim*.

7 Ellmann, *James Joyce*, p. 178. The number of years was reduced in *Ulysses* (p. 249) to coincide with the gestation of the *Portrait:* "Dublin 1904, Trieste 1914."

8 Ellmann, *James Joyce*, pp. 238–39.

9 *Finnegans Wake*, p. 112.

10 See the decision of the United States District Court included in *Ulysses*, pp. vii–xii.

11 See "The Day of the Rabblement" in *The Critical Writings*, pp. 68–72.

12 Ellmann, *James Joyce*, p. 51.

13 Robert Scholes and Richard M. Kain, eds., *The Workshop of Daedalus, James Joyce and the Raw Materials for "A Portrait of the Artist as a Young Man"* Evanston, Ill.: Northwestern University Press, 1965), pp. 11–51. Reprinted in *A Portrait of the Artist as a Young Man*, ed. Chester Anderson (New York: Viking Press, 1968), pp. 257–66.

14 Ellmann, *James Joyce*, p. 169.

15 Scholes, *The Workshop of Daedalus*, p. 60.

16 *The Critical Writings*, p. 71.

17 Scholes, *The Workshop of Daedalus*, p. 60. His actual words are important: ". . . a portrait is not an identificative paper but rather the curve

of an emotion." This idea, derived probably from the French literary historian Hippolyte Taine, implies a steady development along determined lines, a development resulting from a combination of nature and nurture and marked by choices freely made but determined by the bent and capacities of the individual.

Chapter II: Dublin, June 16, 1904

1 This position contradicts the accepted view that Molly is an experienced and hardened adultress, a view which renders Bloom's distress incomprehensible, undercuts the significance of Molly's monologue, and weakens the coherence and narrative structure of *Ulysses*. However, independently of each other, Robert Martin Adams (*"Ulysses"*: *Surface and Symbol* [New York: Oxford University Press, 1962], pp. 35-43) and Stanley Sultan (*The Argument of "Ulysses,"* [Columbus: Ohio State University Press, 1964], pp. 431-34) have demonstrated Molly's relative chastity. Though this point is generally accepted today, it proved distressing when I argued it in detail in "The Empirical Molly" shortly after the appearance of this book in 1970. (Thomas F. Staley and Bernard Benstock, eds., *Approaches to "Ulysses": Ten Essays* [Pittsburgh: University of Pittsburgh Press, 1970], pp. 103-35.) For reactions and polemics, see Nathan Halper's review (in *James Joyce Quarterly* 9, no. 1 [Fall 1971]. 164-67) and my exchange with Darcy O'Brien (in *James Joyce Quarterly* 9, no. 4 [Summer 1972]: 490-94).

2 It may well be that Stephen's remark reflects his befuddled recollection of an event that took place sixteen years earlier at Clongowes school, but the absence of glasses is a significant datum, as is the condition of Stephen's eyes on this special/ordinary day.

3 It is characteristic of Joyce's irony that the tower built to keep the French out of Ireland houses the dilettante Mulligan and the francophile Stephen.

4 *Portrait*, p. 172.

5 Frank Budgen, *James Joyce and the Making of "Ulysses,"* rev. ed. (Bloomington: Indiana University Press, 1960), p. 45.

6 The passage in question is controversial, being associated by many critics with urination, but the case for some sort of auto-eroticism is made in my "Stephen on the Rocks" (in *James Joyce Quarterly* 15, no. 1 [Fall 1977]: 5-17).

7 In "Nestor," when Deasy says, "You have two copies there. If you can have them published at once," Stephen automatically thinks, *"Telegraph, Irish Homestead"* (*Ulysses*, p. 35).

8 When the funeral procession passes Boylan during "Hades," Bloom

covers his embarrassment in a similar way: "Mr Bloom reviewed the nails of his left hand, then those of his right hand" (*Ulysses,* p. 92).

9 For a comprehensive discussion of Joyce's method and sources, see William M. Schutte, *Joyce and Shakespeare: A Study in the Meaning of "Ulysses"* (New Haven: Yale University Press, 1957).

10 There is an unmistakable echo here of the Marquess of Queensberry, the brutal father of Oscar Wilde's lover, Lord Alfred Douglas, and the cause of Wilde's perdition. Joyce has ironically altered this suggestive circumstance, as he has all others.

11 For a full account of their addresses and his jobs, see Molly's monologue (*Ulysses,* p. 772).

12 Bloom's Masonic connections, which function as a parallel for Athena's protection of Ulysses, might help explain the edge he seems to have on the other Jews in the book. But we may question the existence of these connections.

13 The reference is to Dan Dawson's speech, which gets short shrift even from the journalists.

14 Implicit in this image is the view that it would take a combination of two natures to make a Shakespeare for our times. But since we move quickly from an identity of opposites to a father-son relationship, it is worth noting the role played by Shakespeare in the view of Stephen as Bloom's spiritual son. By a sort of metempsychosis ("O, rocks! . . . Tell us in plain words," Molly-Calypso says [64].), Joyce links Shakespeare, who lost an eleven-year-old son, Hamnet, to Bloom, whose son, dead at eleven days, would now be almost eleven, to Stephen, who is now twenty-two but who met Bloom eleven years ago.

15 For a fuller treatment of the farcical component of this chapter and the book as a whole, see my "Forms of Folly in Joyce: A Study of Clowning in *Ulysses*" (in *ELH* 34 [June 1967]: 260-83). Both Hugh Kenner and Marilyn French have written extensive and original studies of this chapter. (See "Circe" in Clive Hart and David Hayman, eds., *James Joyce's "Ulysses": Critical Essays* [Berkeley: University of California Press, 1974], pp. 341-62; *The Book as World: James Joyce's "Ulysses"* [Cambridge: Harvard University Press, 1967], pp. 185-206.)

Chapter III: Two Characters and a City-Scape

1 Arnold Goldman, *The Joyce Paradox: Form and Freedom in His Fiction* (Evanston, Ill.: Northwestern University Press, 1966). Though I would question Joyce's use of Kierkegaard as a source, this view is helpful in distinguishing between Stephen's and Bloom's modes.

2 See especially Adams, *"Ulysses": Surface and Symbol.*

3 The first of these was taken by Joyce from his collection of epiphanies (see Scholes and Kain, *Workshop of Daedalus,* p. 31) and carefully altered to fit the circumstance. See the reference to "harpy" and "bloodless" and the dumbshow effect.

4 The historical Dodd was not Jewish, but the text lets us believe along with Dublin that he was.

5 Amusingly, after Joyce's death, the original for this original, Dr. Oliver St. John Gogarty, accused Joyce, his recreator, of perpetrating a hoax on the world when he wrote *Ulysses* and called Joyce an "artist" in just this sense.

6 Here he is faithful to his model, who was thought to resemble his fellow Oxonian as an Irish wit and promising poet and who, like Wilde, was "stately, plump."

7 In *Finnegans Wake,* the mocker, Shaun the post, says of his artist twin that he has written the darkness out of himself into a universal book very much like the one we would expect Stephen to write (and those Joyce wrote): ". . . and the first till last alshemist wrote over every square inch of the only foolscap available, his own body, till by its corrosive sublimation one continuous present tense integument slowly unfolded all marryvoising moodmoulded cyclewheeling history . . . but with each word that would not pass away the squidself which he had squirtscreened from the crystalline world waned chagreenold and doriangrayer in its dudhud" (*Finnegans Wake,* pp. 185–86).

8 *Portrait,* p. 247.

Chapter IV: Adjuncts to Meaning

1 Budgen, *James Joyce,* pp. 16–17.

2 *Ibid.,* p. 20.

3 Joyce's list of "Correspondences" is incomplete. His Proteus, for example, is "Primal Matter" while his Menelaus is Kevin Egan. No mention is made of Uncle Richie, who is Menelaus as host, or of Stephen, who is Menelaus fighting protean flux. See appendix I.

4 Stuart Gilbert, *James Joyce's "Ulysses"* (New York: Random House, Inc., Vintage Books, 1955), pp. 65–76.

5 For a discussion of this and other aspects of the Shakespeare parallel, see Schutte, *Joyce and Shakespeare,* pp. 18–20 and *passim.*

6 "Is he an old man or a young man? Where are his home and family? . . . And he can't be complete because he's never alone" (Budgen, *James Joyce,* p. 16).

7 Ellmann, *James Joyce,* p. 275.

8 This image is consistent with a statement he makes to himself in "Scylla," where, a doctor among the doct, he reacts to a Wagner-like

Mr Best: "Wit. You would give your five wits for youth's proud livery he pranks in" (*Ulysses*, p. 199).

9 Gilbert, *James Joyce's "Ulysses,"* p. 320–23.

10 For a review of these positions and their application, see William York Tindall, *James Joyce: His Way of Interpreting the Modern World* (New York: Charles Scribner's Sons, 1950). See also Samuel Beckett's perceptive article, "Dante . . . Bruno. Vico . . Joyce" in Samuel Beckett, *et al.*, *Our Exagmination Round his Factification for Incamination of "Work in Progress"* (Norfolk, Va.: New Directions, 1939). What these writers have to say about Bruno and *Finnegans Wake* can in some measure be applied to *Ulysses*.

11 The immediate reference is to Paddy Dignam, dying and dead.

12 "Jewgreek is greekjew. Extremes meet. Death is the highest form of life. Bah!" (*Ulysses*, p. 504). This is an obvious reference to Stephen's meeting with Bloom and their opposite identity, but it also refers to the Judeo-Hellenic nature of our heritage and doubtless to one of Stephen's theories. Typically, the source of the remark is ambiguous. It is assigned to Lynch's cap, but it may be Stephen's hallucination, a mode of self-criticism.

13 *Ulysses*, p. 213.

14 Richard Ellmann (*James Joyce*, p. 351) notes the similarity between this statement and Croce's précis of the work of another of Joyce's favorite philosophers, Giambattista Vico's *The New Science*. Apparently Stephen is moving from one predilection to another in his ceaseless effort to define his predicament.

15 Goldman, *The Joyce Paradox*, p. 158.

16 Clive Hart, *James Joyce's "Ulysses"* (Sydney, Australia: Sydney University Press, 1968), p. 73.

17 A reference to the affair Milly has begun with Bannon.

18 Here both the affair now beginning with Boylan and the resumption of sex with Molly are alluded to.

19 See this in relation to Stephen's response to Deasy's appeal to justice before generosity: "I fear those big words . . . which make us so unhappy" (*Ulysses*, p. 31).

20 See also the stellar sign Stephen claims appeared at Shakespeare's birth (*Ulysses*, p. 210) and his image of the falling Lucifer (*Ibid.*, p. 50).

21 Hart, *James Joyce's "Ulysses,"* pp. 74–75.

Chapter V: Form and Surface

1 S. L. Goldberg, *James Joyce* (New York: Grove Press, 1962), p. 95.

2 See Richard Ellmann, ed., *Letters of James Joyce* (New York: Viking Press, 1966), 2: 409. For a discussion of the technique, see Melvin J.

Friedman, *Stream of Consciousness: a Study of Literary Method* (New Haven: Yale University Press, 1956), pp. 210–43, and Robert Humphrey, *Stream of Consciousness in the Modern Novel* (Berkeley: University of California Press, 1954), *passim*. Robert H. Deming gives two pages of further reading on the subject in *A Bibliography of James Joyce Studies* (Lawrence: University of Kansas Libraries, 1964), pp. 110–11.

3 *Finnegans Wake,* p. 613.

4 Joyce took obvious pleasure in identifying the history of the Irish and the Jews, two conquered nations originating in opposite corners of the West and spreading out in opposite directions in exile and non-nationhood.

5 *Portrait,* p. 50.

6 In connection with these first six chapters, it is worth recalling Stephen's and Joyce's theory of modes:

> The lyrical form is in fact, the simplest verbal vesture of an instant of emotion. . . . He who utters it is more conscious of the instant of emotion than of himself as feeling emotion. The simplest epical form is seen emerging out of lyrical literature when the artist prolongs and broods upon himself as the centre of an epical event and this form progresses till the centre of emotional gravity is equidistant from the artist himself and from others. The narrative is no longer purely personal. The personality of the artist passes into the narration itself flowing round and round the persons and the action. . . . The dramatic form is reached when the vitality which has flowed and eddied around each person fills every person with such vital force that he or she assumes a proper and intangible esthetic life. (*Portrait,* pp. 214–15)

> Substituting the word character for the term "artist," we find that Stephen's chapters roughly approximate the movement from "dramatic" to "lyric" while Bloom's, operating in the comic rather than the serious or romantic mode, move from lyrical to dramatic in the proper order. Joyce appears to be checking out ironically his own theory.

7 Significantly, Stephen is called "Mocker" here, an identity generally reserved for Mulligan.

8 This strategy, together with an almost dickensian treatment of character and incident, was taken over by Virginia Woolf in her first experimental effort, *Mrs. Dalloway,* in which a pair of motifs unites people from all walks in various parts of Westminster at a given hour of the morning.

9 Constantine P. Curran, *James Joyce Remembered* (New York: Oxford University Press, 1968), p. 29.

10 The gross and powerful image of irremediable sterility that punctuates Bloom's vision does not preclude the appeal to the spiritual East or the validity of the life image, though, like the actual cloud that inspires it, it casts both in shadow.

11 In this connection, see little Rudy in lambswool.

12 It is characteristic of Stephen that though he too uses Dryden's words ("Cousin Swift, you will never be a poet"), unlike Mulligan, he applies them with significant alteration to himself in a protean context: "Cousin Stephen, you will never be a saint" (*Ulysses*, p. 40).

13 See also the description of the key and lock as a male-female couple in "Ithaca," p. 703.

14 The fact that this refers to the aria *"Tutto è sciolto"* deepens and trivializes Bloom's meaning, underlining both his lack of originality and his inability to express his anguish. For further comment on Joyce's use of musical allusion in "Sirens," see Weldon Thornton, *Allusions in "Ulysses"* (Chapel Hill: University of North Carolina Press, 1968).

Ten Years After Thoughts

1 See David Mayer, *Harlequin in His Element* (Cambridge: Harvard University Press, 1969).

2 Both in Hugh Kenner's *Joyce's Voices* (Berkeley: University of California Press, 1978) and his more recent and advanced *"Ulysses"* (London: George Allen and Unwin, 1980).

3 *Portrait,* p. 216. Cited by Kenner in *"Ulysses,"* p. 68 (his italics).

4 Or what Dorrit Cohn brilliantly treats under "narrated monologue" in *Transparent Minds* (Princeton: Princeton University Press, 1978), pp. 109-13 and *passim.*

5 Michael Groden, *"Ulysses" in Progress* (Princeton: Princeton University Press, 1977), pp. 114-65.

6 In defense of this position, Hugh Kenner notes in his *Ulysses* (pp. 62-63) that the opening sentence of "Aeolus" was clearly obtrusive and arbitrary even before Joyce thought to interpolate the newspaper headlines. The earliest existing typescript began "Grossbooted draymen rolled barrels dullthudding out of Prince's stores and bumped them up the brewery float." To this Joyce then added "on the brewery float bumped dullthudding barrels rolled by grossbooted draymen out of Prince's stores." (See Michael Groden, ed., *The James Joyce Archive* [New York: Garland Publishing, 1978], *James Joyce "Ulysses": Notes & "Telemachus"—"Scylla and Charybdis"* p. 286). The typescript page contains even more striking evidence of arrangement: "Mr Bloom turned and saw the liveried porter raise his lettered cap as a stately figure entered from Prince's street. Dullthudding Guinness' barrels."

(Kenner, *"Ulysses,"* p. 17). Neither the initial sentence of the draft nor this curious recall belongs to the established narrator. Both bear witness to the early presence of the arranger and such evidence can be multiplied.

7 David Hayman, "Stephen on the Rocks," *James Joyce Quarterly* 15, no. 1 (Fall 1977): pp. 5–17.

8 This view has been challenged. See Herbert Schneidau's "One Eye and Two Levels: On Joyce's 'Cyclops' " and my "Two Eyes at Two Levels: A Response to Herbert Schneidau on Joyce's 'Cyclops' " in *James Joyce Quarterly* 16, nos. 1/2 (Fall 1978/Winter 1979): 95–110. See also C. H. Peake, *James Joyce: The Citizen and the Artist* (Stanford: Stanford University Press, 1977), pp. 234–35, who, like Schneidau, sees the monologue as taking place in the persona's mind during the action and claims that the parenthetical asides are in fact his stream of consciousness. But Paul P. J. van Caspel (*Bloomers on the Liffey: Eisegetical Readings of James Joyce's "Ulysses" Part II* [Groningen: Venstra Visser Offset, 1980], pp. 213–16 and *passim*), adduces other arguments in support of a double temporality.

9 For a fuller treatment of this material and justification of these conclusions, see my "Cyclops" in *James Joyce's "Ulysses": Critical Essays,* Clive Hart and David Hayman, eds. (Berkeley: University of California Press, 1974), pp. 243–76. A suggestive treatment of the asides is given by Peake, pp. 236–42, whose reading of the chapter, like much of his book, tends otherwise to be heavily moralistic.

10 "The Empirical Molly" in *Approaches to "Ulysses": Ten Essays,* Thomas F. Staley and Bernard Benstock, eds. (Pittsburgh: University of Pittsburgh Press, 1970), pp. 103–35.

11 A fuller but still tentative treatment of this and related topics will appear as "Insets in Joyce" in a forthcoming volume edited by Hugh Kenner and Thomas F. Staley.

12 I have treated it in a forthcoming article for the French publication *Cahiers de l'Herne,* ed. Jacques Aubert and Fritz Senn, under the title "James Joyce Paratactician."

Bibliography

Primary Sources

The following works are not cited in the text. For further information on the Joyce canon, see J. J. Slocum and Herbert Cahoon, *A Bibliography of James Joyce, 1882–1941,* New Haven: Yale University Press, 1953.

Chamber Music. Edited by William York Tindall. New York: Columbia University Press, 1954.

Dubliners. Edited by Robert Scholes and A. Walton Litz. New York: Viking Press, 1969.

Exiles. New York: Viking Press, 1951.

Giacomo Joyce. Edited by Richard Ellmann. New York: Viking Press, 1968.

Stephen Hero. New York: New Directions, 1963. (Augmented text.)

Letters of James Joyce. 3 vols. Vol. 1, edited by Stuart Gilbert. New York: Viking Press, 1957. Vols. 2 and 3, edited by Richard Ellmann, New York: Viking Press, 1966.

Selected Letters. Edited by Richard Ellmann. New York: Viking Press, 1975. (Contains materials not included in the earlier volumes.)

Secondary Sources

The following highly selective list updates the *Ulysses* bibliography. It does not include all of the items referred to in my text and footnotes or any of the large number of fine essays which have appeared throughout the decades. For a balanced assessment of critical perspectives, see Clive Hart's *James Joyce's "Ulysses"* (Sydney: Sydney University Press, 1968) and especially the survey by Thomas F. Staley in Richard J. Finneran's *Anglo-Irish Literature: A Review of Research* (New York: Modern Language Association, 1976), pp. 366–435. The most comprehensive bibliography is Robert Deming's *A Bibliography of James Joyce Studies* (2d ed., rev. and enl. [Boston: G. K. Hall, 1977]). Supplementary checklists can be found in numbers of the *James Joyce Quarterly* and in the annual bibliography of *PMLA*.

Adams, Robert M. *Surface and Symbol: The Consistency of James Joyce's "Ulysses."* New York: Oxford University Press, 1962.

Benstock, Bernard, and Shari Benstock. *Who's He When He's at Home: A James Joyce Directory.* Urbana: University of Illinois Press, 1980.

Bonnerot, Louis, ed. *"Ulysses": Cinquante ans après: témoignages Franco-Anglais sur le chef-d'oeuvre de James Joyce.* Paris: Didier, 1974. (With many essays in English.)

Budgen, Frank. *James Joyce and the Making of "Ulysses."* Bloomington: Indiana University Press, 1960.

Burgess, Anthony. *Joysprick: an Introduction to the Language of James Joyce.* New York: Harcourt Brace, 1973.

Cohn, Dorrit. *Transparent Minds: Narrative Modes for Presenting Consciousness in Fiction.* Princeton: Princeton University Press, 1978.

Cope, Jackson. *Joyce's Cities: Archeologies of the Soul.* Baltimore: The Johns Hopkins University Press, 1981.

Curran, Constantine. *James Joyce Remembered.* New York: Oxford University Press, 1968.

Ellmann, Richard. *James Joyce.* New York: Oxford University Press, 1959.

Ellmann, Richard. *The Consciousness of James Joyce.* New York: Oxford University Press, 1977.

French, Marilyn. *The Book as World: James Joyce's "Ulysses."* Cambridge: Harvard University Press, 1976.

Gifford, Don, and Robert J. Seidman. *Notes for Joyce: an Annotation of James Joyce's "Ulysses."* New York: Dutton, 1974.

Gilbert, Stuart. *James Joyce's "Ulysses": A Study.* New York: Knopf, 1952.

Goldberg, S. L. *The Classical Temper.* New York: Barnes and Noble, 1961.

Goldman, Arnold. *The Joyce Paradox: Form and Freedom in His Fiction.* Evanston: Northwestern University Press, 1966.

Gose, Elliot B., Jr. *The Transformation Process in "Ulysses."* Toronto: University of Toronto Press, 1980.

Groden, Michael. *"Ulysses" in Progress.* Princeton: Princeton University Press, 1977.

Groden, Michael, ed. *The James Joyce Archive.* 63 vols. See especially the volumes on *James Joyce "Ulysses."* New York: Garland Publishing, 1978.

Hart, Clive. *James Joyce's "Ulysses."* Sydney: Sydney University Press, 1968.

Hart, Clive, and David Hayman, eds. *James Joyce's "Ulysses": Critical Essays.* Berkeley: University of California Press, 1974.

Hart, Clive, and Leo Knuth. *A Topographical Guide to James Joyce's "Ulysses."* Colchester: A Wake Newslitter Press, 1975.

Herring, Phillip, ed. *Joyce's "Ulysses" Notesheets in the British Museum.* Charlottesville: University Press of Virginia, 1972.

Herring, Phillip, ed. *Joyce's Notes and Early Drafts for "Ulysses": Selections from the Buffalo Collection.* Charlottesville: University Press of Virginia, 1977.

Iser, Wolfgang. *The Implied Reader: Patterns of Communication in Prose Fiction from Bunyan to Beckett.* Baltimore: The Johns Hopkins University Press, 1974.

Kenner, Hugh. *Dublin's Joyce.* Bloomington: Indiana University Press, 1956.

Kenner, Hugh. *Joyce's Voices.* Berkeley: University of California Press, 1978.

Kenner, Hugh. *"Ulysses".* London: George Allen and Unwin, 1980.

Litz, A. Walton. *The Art of James Joyce: Method and Design in "Ulysses" and "Finnegans Wake."* New York: Oxford University Press, 1961.

Maddox, James H., Jr. *Joyce's "Ulysses" and the Assault upon Character.* New Brunswick, N.J.: Rutgers University Press, 1978.

Peake, C. H. *James Joyce: The Citizen and the Artist.* Stanford: Stanford University Press, 1977.

Potts, Willard. *Portraits of the Artist in Exile: Recollections of James Joyce by Europeans.* Seattle: University of Washington Press, 1979.

Raleigh, John Henry. *The Chronicle of Leopold and Molly Bloom: "Ulysses" as Narrative.* Berkeley: University of California Press, 1977.

Staley, Thomas F., ed. *"Ulysses": Fifty Years.* Bloomington: Indiana University Press, 1974.

Staley, Thomas F., and Bernard Benstock, eds. *Approaches to "Ulysses": Ten Essays.* Pittsburgh: University of Pittsburgh Press, 1970.

Sultan, Stanley. *The Argument of "Ulysses."* Columbus: Ohio State University Press, 1965.

Thornton, Weldon. *Allusions in "Ulysses."* Chapel Hill: University of North Carolina Press, 1968.

Van Caspel, Paul P. J. *Bloomers on the Liffey: Eisegetical Readings of James Joyce's "Ulysses" Part II.* Groningen: Veenstra Visser Offset, 1980.

Index

Abbey Theatre, 12
Adams, Robert Martin, 135
AE (George Russell) 12, 16, 29, 96
"Aeolus" (*Ulysses*), 28, 125
  Bloom in, 35, 76
  rhetoric in, 20, 83, 90, 95, 115
  Stephen in, 25, 95-96, 110, 129
"agenbite of inwit," 31, 68, 92, 108
Ajax, 35
analogies:
  in *Portrait*, 17
  in *Ulysses*, 18, 20-21, 37, 61-81,
    83, 101-2
Anthony, Saint, 71, 101
anti-Semitism, 117
  in "Cyclops," 37
  of Deasy, 27, 86
  in Stephen's song, 33, 41
arranger, 88-104, 112, 117, 122-25,
  126
  catechism used by, 103, 132, 133
  chapters balanced by, 84-86, 93, 96
  defined, 84, 122-23
  parallels multiplied by, 86, 97
  style manipulated by, 100-101,
    129-32
Artifoni, Almidano, 30
Athena, 62, 64, 155*n*
auto-eroticism:
  of Bloom, 38, 69, 85, 100
  of Stephen, 28, 85*n*, 126

Balzac, Honoré de, 53
Bannon, 38
Barnacle, Nora, 7
Beach, Sylvia, 10
Beckett, Samuel, 111, 118

Benstock, Bernard, 135
Benstock, Shari, 122, 135
Bérard, Victor, 64
Berlin Alexanderplatz (Döblin), 14
Best, Mr., 56, 90, 97, 157*n*
"Biddy Doran," 10
bird-girl, 25, 85*n*, 111, 126
Bloom, Leopold, 19, 23, 33-42, 45-
  51, 58, 78-81, 110-6, 126
  in "Aeolus," 35, 76
  auto-eroticism, of, 38, 69, 85, 100
  in "Calypso," 33-35, 85, 107
  in "Circe," 36, 38, 70
  as comic figure, 45-51, 72, 95, 98,
    107
  Dignam's funeral and, 22, 35, 37,
    48
  in Dublin community, 52-56
  as father, 31, 35, 38, 40-41, 107
  foils for, 97
  in "Hades," 35, 95, 154*n*
  as Jew, 33-35, 37, 48, 69, 70-71,
    80, 116, 121
  keys/Keyes and, 23, 35, 36, 46, 86,
    114
  in "Lestrygonians," 36, 52, 55
  in "Lotus Eaters," 35, 111-12
  Mulligan and, 36, 38, 66, 70
  as narrator, 47, 101-102
  in "Nausikaa," 23, 38, 85-86, 126
  in "Oxen of the Sun," 31, 38, 47
  prototypes of, 9, 18
  psuedonymous correspondence of,
    34, 35
  as Shakespeare, 34, 36, 40, 48, 69
  as Stephen's opposite, 45, 47-51,
    74-77, 95

165

TEXT DESIGNED BY GARY G. GORE
JACKET DESIGNED BY PHILL THILL
COMPOSED BY THE COMPOSING ROOM
KIMBERLY, WISCONSIN
MANUFACTURED BY BANTA COMPANY
MENASHA, WISCONSIN
TEXT AND DISPLAY LINES ARE SET IN BASKERVILLE

Library of Congress Cataloging in Publication Data
Hayman, David.
Ulysses, the mechanics of meaning.
Bibliography: pp. 161–163.
Includes index.
1. Joyce, James, 1882–1941. Ulysses.
I. Title.
PR6019.09U6544   1982   823'.912   81-70007
ISBN 0-299-09020-5   AACR2
ISBN 0-299-09024-8 (pbk.)